THREE POINTS SHY

THE TRUE STORY OF
**SEMINOLE HIGH'S QUEST FOR THE 1980 FLORIDA
HIGH SCHOOL STATE BASKETBALL CHAMPIONSHIP**

JOE DESANTIS
FOREWORD BY SAM COOK

Published by Lee's Press and Publishing Company
www.LeesPress.net

Lee's PRESS | *A Premiere Self-Publishing Services Company*

This document is published by Lee's Press and Publishing Company located in the United States of America. It is protected by the United States Copyright

Act, all applicable state laws, and international copyright laws. The information in this document is accurate to the best of the ability of Joe DeSantis at the time of writing. The content of this document is subject to change without notice.

Photography by Vic DeSantis/DeSantis Digital Works & DeSantis Photography, Viera, FL.

Permission from the current publisher of *The Sanford Herald*, Susan Wenner

ISBN-13: 9798386574123

HARDBACK

Foreword

The birth of Seminole High's dominance in sports began many years ago. And author Joe DeSantis was there to help chronicle it.

"I've been carrying this story around for 40 years," DeSantis says. "It's such an amazing story of what might have been, should have been, what a-could-a-would-have been. Better sit down and write it while I still can."

DeSantis grew up as a Navy brat bouncing around the world and up and down the U.S. East Coast. He spent time in Alaska, Italy, Virginia, New Jersey, and New Hampshire. As a high school sophomore with no direction, he took Ms. Florence Blankenship's 10th grade English class. She poked him to become a writer. During a Parent/Teacher Conference, she told his parents, "He has potential if he would only come to class." (He was a notorious class skipper).

As a sports editor, DeSantis wanted his sports pages of *The Sanford Herald* to reflect that potential. He convinced, cajoled, and persuaded the newspaper's management to get on board and forged a supportive relationship with managing editor, Tom Giordano. Between that magical Seminole High basketball season of 1979, and for years to come, he developed the blueprint for local sports coverage. There was no doubt DeSantis was taking charge of the operation.

During this time, I worked as a local high school sports stringer and reporter for DeSantis. I learned much from him and his organization from techniques to enthusiasm. When I eventually became sports editor at *The Sanford Herald*, I continued DeSantis' legacy.

i

Yet, the author of this book went on to other journalistic endeavors. He departed *The Sanford Herald* in 1982 to return to his hometown of Erie, Pa. where he helped a fledging Erie Cardinals baseball team get started in the New York Penn League. He finally finished his college degree in between sports seasons at the Edinboro University of Pennsylvania.

And to indicate how life comes full circle, he later returned to Central Florida and worked at *The Sanford Herald* as a county government beat writer and an adjunct communications faculty member at Seminole State College.

In the spring of 2022, DeSantis began writing his book, fixated on colorful memories of that 1979-80 basketball season. Magically, he was able to reconnect with Seminole High coach Bill Payne, now retired in the northwestern hills of North Carolina. In gathering information for this book, the author and the coach spent numerous Sunday afternoons in recollective conversations on the phone proving that great seasons can have great memories, even if your team comes up three points shy.

DeSantis' insight into the quest of Coach Bill Payne's basketball players provides an inspirational look into the journey of a spectacular coach and his team. ---*Sam Cook*

Acknowledgments

In writing the manuscript for "Three Points Shy," the author has utilized personal memories, his notes, as well as previously published facts about the events of this novel written by him and fellow sports department members of *The Sanford Herald*. Conversations with some of the principals in the story, and the microfilm archives of *The Sanford Herald* during his tenure as sports editor have also been incorporated.

Previously published game story accounts, in part or in whole, now more than four decades old, are republished with permission of the current publisher of *The Sanford Herald*, Susan Wenner, and with the support and encouragement of 1979-1982 sports department colleagues Sam Cook and Benton Wood.

Dedication

"Three Points Shy" is dedicated in part to the memory of Ms. Florence Blankenship, for years a beloved English and Journalism teacher and faculty sponsor of the student newspaper "The Roundtable" at Floyd E. Kellam High in Va. Beach, where I first began to write. Ms. Blankenship introduced me to journalism, provided me the opportunity to earn my first byline, and sparked my career that would span more than 40 years in print and broadcast journalism. She also gave me a good swift kick in the pants my sophomore year when I needed a little "guidance."

The novel is also dedicated to the countless high school coaches and athletic directors in Seminole County during the period I served as sports editor of *The Sanford Herald*. They worked untold hours for small stipends and treated our sports staff with professional respect, were always supportive of our efforts to cover their teams which, in turn, contributed greatly to the success of our local coverage.

And finally, this book is dedicated to all the high school student-athletes, past, and present, who take the time, put in the work, and make the sacrifices necessary to represent their teams, schools, and communities.

Table of Contents

Introduction

"Three Points Shy" is the season-long journey of one of the greatest high school teams in the history of Seminole County, Florida.

Coached by skilled tactician and savvy motivator Bill Payne, and led by seniors Bruce McCray, Reggie Butler, David Thomas, Keith Whitney, and Glenn Stambaugh, the Fighting Seminoles of Sanford High would punctuate their record-breaking season with a 1979-80 run at Florida's Class 4A State Basketball Championship.

Their journey would be filled with a combination of dominating wins, last-second heroics, mid-season heartache, and final stretch redemption.

Along the way, there would be holiday tournament championship trophies and three incredible showdowns with the one team that stood in their way of making it to the Lakeland Civic Center's Final Four—Daytona Beach Mainland.

Rarely were two high school teams who played in the same conference ranked among the state's top 5 in Florida's High School Prep Polls. And each of the three meetings between Seminole and Daytona Beach Mainland would provide for a roller coaster ride of emotions, soul-crushing shortcomings, and ultimately a decisive measure of Sanford High's heart and mettle as a basketball team.

The Fighting Seminoles would capture and carry the hopes of their small Central Florida town through a gritty season of winning streaks, setbacks, and comebacks. And along the way, the story of their starters and reserves on the bench would play out on the sports pages of *The Sanford Herald,* the local paper that chronicled each step of their journey.

They would break school records and total the most victories ever in a single high school basketball season in Seminole County. At times, they would have their hearts broken as well. And there would be heart-warming sacrifices from unsuspected sources as part of their journey.

"Three Points Shy" is an enjoyable read for anyone even remotely connected to high school sports programs. It provides a game-by-game insight into the success, failure, and character of student-athletes who don the uniforms of their respective teams to represent their schools and communities. And it is a testament to the coaches who lead them and the fans who follow them.

CHAPTER 1
Hoops, Hopes, and Dreams

"Jesus, I hate this part more than anything," Bill Payne thought.

"How do you tell these young kids they didn't make it, they're just not good enough, they're not wanted?"

In a few minutes, Seminole High School's coach would perform the singular task almost every prep basketball coach despised: posting the roster for the upcoming season outside the men's locker room entrance. Almost as difficult as selecting the players who would suit up for the season soon to unfold, was the delicate responsibility of eliminating dozens of hopefuls who would not make the team.

Compounding the task for Payne and countless high school coaches like him, was the fact that after weeks of tryouts and drills, he would have to face many of those on the cut list eye-to-eye in the days and weeks ahead as they sat as students in the Health and Physical Education classes he taught at Seminole High School.

He would do as he had done in the past, tell kids not quite good enough to earn a jersey and number that represented their school and community, that he still loved them, cared about them, and supported them.

His annual chore of trimming the roster was buffered somewhat as he chuckled back to his first day on campus two seasons prior. Hired away from Colonial High in nearby Orlando's incredibly tough and talented Metro Conference, Payne would be the new face of Seminole High basketball and the freshest coach in The Five Star Conference, comprised of some of the largest schools split between Seminole and Volusia counties.

3

He inherited a program down on its luck with few winning seasons in recent memory. And his first day at his new job was anything but reassuring that fortunes would positively turn in short order.

It was late in the summer of 1977 when he first reported to the campus in the heart of Sanford.

Payne didn't even have keys to the gym and was let into the facility by head football coach and Seminole High Athletic Director Jerry Posey. His cramped office was Spartanly furnished. A metal desk, archaic chair, a telephone, one filing cabinet, and one lonely ball rack containing six forlorn Wilson basketballs, each in worse shape than the other. The leather balls beaten down to the nubs to Payne surprisingly still held air.

To keep high school kids off the streets and ostensibly out of trouble, the Florida High School Athletic Associated permitted high schools to open their gyms during summer break and let the neighborhood kids come and play—just as long as there were no (wink-wink) "organized practices" or anything resembling "coaching" going on.

Payne rolled the ball cart out into the gym adjacent to his cubby hole where dozens of young kids were waiting. The attendees, mostly Black kids with a few white faces sprinkled in, scarfed up the balls and quickly organized themselves into half-court five-on-fives. The rag-tag assembly knew the unofficial rules of summer break gym ball. "You got next" was the law of the land, and whoever didn't get on the court during the first round of games was penciled in to play the winners of the first teams to 21 points. They would play until their legs fell off, or they lost interest, or a combination of the two.

4

Payne ducked back into his office to unpack his personal coach's belongings, hang a few pieces of sports memorabilia on the office's cinderblock walls, and place a few phone calls.

Two hours later, he returned to the gym to find it empty and soundless. Every one of the kids was gone and so were all six weather-beaten basketballs.

"Well, this is interesting," a bemused Payne said out loud. Undaunted, he wheeled the empty ball rack back into his office and locked it for safekeeping.

Seminole High's new hoops coach returned to the gym the following morning, greeted by the same group of faces he found in the gym on day one, with maybe a few more curious kids on hand to see what this new coach was all about.

Payne again wheeled the ball rack out from his office and presented its naked contents to the group.

"Gentlemen, we have one small problem," he mildly barked.

"No basketballs, no gym time."

Payne eyed the group up and down and they in return eyed him. No one spoke or offered a remedy to the situation. After 30 seconds of mutual stare-down, the coach quietly wheeled around and stepped back into his office.

One minute went by. Another transpired. Still silence from the gym. Yet a third minute ticked by, and still not a sound. Payne eyed his watch and began to hear it at minute number four. First came the muffled sound of one ball meeting the gym floor. Then his coach's ear could pick up the sound of a second ball bouncing. Shortly a third joined the noise and then a fourth.

5

Later that afternoon, his second day on the job, Payne returned to the gym. The ball rack on wheels was parked squarely in the center court jump circle. On it were four of the erstwhile and previously absent basketballs.

Payne scoped out the empty gym, casually strolled over to the ball rack, and began to wheel it to its safe haven once again.

He allowed himself a small grin and chuckled.

"Four is not six, but we've made at least a little progress," he thought.

Now, two years later, in the Fall of 1979, Payne was entering his third season.

Formal tryouts had been completed and with the usual wait time to see which football players would help fill out his roster, Payne's team for that year was all but set.

The starting five for his senior-dominated squad had grown and improved significantly over the first two seasons. Payne was pleased with his supporting cast and knew his bench would play an undetermined, but significant role in their quest for a Five Star Conference title and District 9 playoff berth.

Among the group of reserves was senior guard Mike Gaudreau, whose selfless gesture on the very day of the District Tournament later that season literally and figuratively saved Seminole High's State Championship run. Fresh from the recently concluded football season, Joe Baker would be a bruising force as a backup forward. When Joe Baker drove into the paint, it was wise not to stand in his way. Shun Thomas, another senior with solid all-around skills, would serve as the team's sixth man and usually the first off the bench in Payne's substitute rotation. Steve Grace, one of the few white players on the squad, would spell starting center

6

Reggie Butler in the paint. Grace would be smart enough to earn an appointment to the U.S. Naval Academy and talented enough to suit up for the Midshipmen's basketball team following his graduation from Sanford's Seminole High. Robert Guy, Fred Alexander, Clarence Sippio, Willie White, and Casey Jones would add depth and length to Payne's starting five.

But it was Seminole High's starters that Payne would lean on heavily to navigate the '79-80 season.

As junior varsity players, this nucleus paid their dues in the Five Star Conference with just a handful of wins. Payne had nurtured this group to an improved 14-11 season as juniors, good enough for a third-place conference finish.

As their senior season was about to unfold in the always-tough Conference and District 9 play, Payne's gut told him he had some horses. Not one to count his chickens, in the early days of the basketball pre-season, he was cautiously optimistic this year had the potential to be something special. He was also aware that Five Star Conference rivals that included Deland, Longwood Lyman, Lake Howell, and Lake Brantley among others were like navigating a minefield with a blindfold on. Nobody would roll over and play dead for his Sanford team. Further down the road, there would be two critical encounters with Daytona Beach Mainland, forty minutes away. Like Seminole High, the Buccaneers had been building for the past two seasons. And likewise, the troops of rival coach Dick Toth were considered by many around the state of Florida as the pre-season number one team with a realistic shot at a Class 4-A State Championship. Payne purposely scheduled a home-and-home encounter with Evans High that season as well. Maynard Evans High was a perennial contender from that incredibly deep and talented Orlando hotbed of both basketball and football. The

7

Metro Conference routinely produced teams that made deep and serious runs at 4-A Class state basketball championships. It was a familiar pitstop for college recruiters around the state. At the very least, the two games against the Evans Trojans, where Darryl Dawkins of "Chocolate Thunder" fame led the Trojans to the 1975 Class 4-A state title loomed, as did home-and-home contests against the Metro's Boone Braves who advanced to the 1977 state semifinals in Lakeland as well as Edgewater, another Metro team that made it to the Final Four in 1976. Winter Park was also on the schedule, yet another Metro Conference team that made it to the 1974 Championship game, losing to a Miami Jackson team later declared ineligible. It was safe to say that Payne scheduled no patsies outside the Five Star Conference competition and positioned his team for some early schedule seasoning and a good barometer of how good they might be. If anything, the 1979 calendar leading up to traditional Christmas break time would be an early litmus test, helping determine if his talented Seminole squad might be prepared enough to sail Seminole High basketball into the uncharted waters of post-season play.

Even with the traditional strength of the neighboring Metro Conference, Seminole High and Daytona Beach Mainland would quietly but quickly become the epicenter of high school basketball that season in Central Florida. And both schools took on the nuances of the communities they represented.

Constructed in 1961, Seminole High was nestled along Ridgewood Avenue, a short distance from the southern banks of Lake Monroe, leading to the pathway of the St. Johns River.

Sanford, Florida's history was an enigma of small-town beginnings, including periodic racial strife and the good and bad that came with growing up in the shadows of Walt Disney World. Like the nearby cities of Longwood, Casselberry, Altamonte Springs, Fern Park, Winter Springs, and Oviedo, Sanford took on its role as one of many Central Florida bedroom communities to Orlando, bursting at the seams in 1979.

The landscape at adjacent Daytona Beach was a world apart from Sanford. Riding the sun-soaked shores of the Atlantic Ocean in Daytona Beach and nearby Holly Hill, most white kids hit the beach and surfed; most Black kids played basketball. Exceptionally well.

Nicknamed "Celery City" for its prominent position in Florida's agricultural landscape, Sanford was the quintessential paradox of small-town Florida. The same small town played a supporting role in railroad development in the deep south. It once held a strategic military position as a Naval Air Station. But even in 1979, it was a town that took on the persona of bipolar twins.

To borrow from Charles Dickens, Sanford in 1979 truly remained a Tale of Two Cities. In the worst of times, it was a southern town whose 1946 police chief Roy G. Williams ran baseball icon Jackie Robinson out of town when he attempted to play in a minor league game at a city park because the town didn't permit racially mixed teams to use athletic facilities. In the best of times, Sanford and surrounding Seminole County would become the stomping grounds of future World Series MVP David Eckstein, future Major League Baseball Hall of Famer Tim Raines, the Boston Red Sox's Jason Varitek, a backstop to a record four Major League no-hitters, and Dave Martinez, a high school Lake Howell Silver Hawk, and MLB veteran who would become manager of the Washington Nationals.

Yet again, Sanford's image and reputation would years hence become embroiled with the worst of times when Black teenager

9

Trayvon Martin encountered white neighborhood self-proclaimed watchdog George Zimmerman on a fateful evening in February of 2012 that resulted in the death of Martin, and the ignominy of both Sanford and Zimmerman played out in a daily televised trial.

And likewise, Sanford would enjoy the best of times when Payne's 1979-80 team made an improbable, record-breaking run in quest of what every high school sports team sets its sights on during the first day of practice in a new season: a state championship.

Payne's senior-dominated roster that season provided the quintessential melding of Sanford's cultural and societal backdrop. Most of his players were Black and hailed from Sanford's Historical Community of Goldsboro, located on the West side of the railroad tracks on Highway 17-92. Homes here were small, modest, cinderblock construction. At the time, there was limited retail, few grocery stores outside of convenience marts, a loose collection of hardscrabble playgrounds, and home to the majority of Sanford's public housing. Those railroad tracks split the town in half. Right next door, but literally and figuratively a world away, sat Sanford's downtown commerce and Historic District to the East. Punctuated with cobblestone streets, store-front businesses, and white-columned houses with wrap-around porches, it comprised the "other half" of Sanford. Seminole County's seat of government was located here as well in 1979, with the Court House a dominating structure along North Park Avenue and a majority of other county offices scattered around the heart of the downtown district.

The Colonial Room Restaurant on East 1st Street was the breakfast gathering place for much of Sanford's business community. Eggs, bacon, grits, toast, and coffee were served in a loud, clattering amalgamation of booths, tables, and swivel bar seats at the counter. The waitresses scrambled each day when breakfast conversations revolved around local business developments, small-town gossip, political rumor, and sports chatter about how the local teams were shaping up for the season.

"The usual order today, Sugar," reflected the familiarity between patrons and wait staff as harried ladies with aproned skirts and hand-held order pads hustled for hot meals and tips.

The Colonial Room would become one of several Sanford eateries offering a "sponsorship" meal for Sanford High's sports teams, when and if they made post-season runs.

By night, and after the games, many of the same breakfast patrons would regather at Wolfy's Lakefront Bar & Grill on North Palmetto to dissect the outcome of Seminole High sports fortunes, second-guess the coaches, nurse their Gin & Tonics, and embellish their athletic accomplishments of "back in the day."

It was against this backdrop that Payne, part coach, mentor, motivator, disciplinarian, father figure, public relations artist, and salesman, tried to gauge his potential for a serious run at Florida's Class 4-A State Basketball Championship—then, the largest school classification for athletics.

He began to jot down notes on a legal pad as he eye-balled his starting five. His synopsis was brief but player-by-player accurate.

At point guard would be Keith Whitney, a solidly built left-handed, 5-10 gizmo with speed to burn, the ability to run Sanford's up-tempo offense, and a capable defender with a decent 10–15-foot jumper. When he played under control, he was the perfect maestro for this senior nucleus.

At shooting guard, an unknown quantity to the Seminole Tribe at

11

the outset of that season. At 6-1, Glenn Stambaugh was a senior transfer who arrived in Payne's lap during the summer. A previous star at neighboring rival Lyman High in Longwood, Stambaugh enrolled at Seminole High with provisions to retain athletic eligibility because Sanford offered academic courses not available at his former school. For Payne, it was like Christmas in July. The only white player among Seminole High's starting five, Stambaugh brought a deadly outside jump shot, capable defense, and ball-handling. He was an assassin from the charity stripe.

Centering Payne's lineup would be Reggie Butler, a tall, angular 6-6 pillar who played like the proverbial Little Girl with The Curl. Usually shy about going to the bucket, Sanford's big man in the paint had the propensity to either be dominant or disappear on a given game night. Butler was fully capable of crashing the boards, playing demonic defense, and chipping in with put-back points on a Tuesday scheduled game. Occasionally, by Friday night's contest, one might have to scout the box score to see if he was in the lineup.

The offensive and defensive heart and soul of Payne's senior lineup sat on the front line in a pair of 6-4 forwards. On one side was the Tribe's leading offensive threat Bruce McCray. Some guys are shooters. Some guys are scorers. McCray was a little of both. He was deadly from 10-15 feet, and when he played under the backboards, he was like a starved pit bull looking for a morsel. Somehow, he consistently rebounded well and picked up a copious amount of "garbage" buckets with any combination from among a group of unorthodox shots from five feet in. Like a football linebacker, he had a nose for the ball and often arrived in the right place at the right time.

Rounding out Payne's starting five for that 1979-80 season was the defensive glue that held this unit together through thick and thin, David Thomas. At a Spiderman 6-4, with great reach and superior launch, Thomas played at 6-10. He often drew the assignment of guarding the opposition's best offensive player, was a man possessed on the boards, could score if, and when he wanted to or needed to, and held the entire team accountable. Thomas was the perfect enigma of the Seminole team that year and of the small town they represented. He could be an ambassador for the game in one moment, the eye in the hurricane of discipline issues and trouble in the next.

This would be the nexus of Seminole High's run for a state title that would take as many twists, turns, and convolutions as the history of the town they represented, Sanford.

Fate, luck, chance, and happenstance would accentuate the wild ride that was about to begin for Sanford's Fighting Seminoles. It was November 1979, and almost time for the first jump ball.

CHAPTER 2
Maximizing Available Resources

Like most sports departments at small daily newspapers in the late 1970s and early 1980s, the Halloween weekend was a blitzkrieg of activity that stretched thin the resources of even the most efficiently managed staff.

That was certainly the case at *The Sanford Herald*, one of the longest-established newspapers in the Central Florida area and the only daily in Seminole County. The newspaper's offices and printing presses sat on the shores of Lake Monroe, housed within a large, prefabricated building with a metal roof. In August and September, when strong afternoon thunderstorms routinely rolled in around 4 p.m., the din of the pounding rain on metal was deafening. Veteran staff tried to schedule phone calls and phone interviews around thundershowers to avoid mother nature's periodic cacophony.

Late October marked high school football playoffs, other fall sports wrap-ups, and the launch of men's and women's prep basketball and other winter sports. Title IX, the Federal Legislation that leveled the playing field for women's sports at high school and college programs, was kicking in, and the ladies demanded equal coverage, taxing sports staff and spreading them thinner than usual.

The sales and administrative offices of *The Sanford Herald* fronted the building facing 17-92 just before it curled around the edge of Lake Monroe and led out to the Central Florida Zoo, up and over a decrepit two-lane bridge, and into DeBary and Volusia County, where some of the Five Star Conference teams called home.

The building was fronted with huge glass windows, and on more

14

than one occasion, then publisher Wayne Doyle found himself dodging palm trees sent crashing through the glass from near hurricane winds that cropped up in late Fall.

Office furnishings were typical of the 1970s, with Formica counter tops, sturdy steel desks, swivel chairs, land-line telephones perched on each reporter's desk, and the glare of overhead fluorescent lighting.

The composition room sat to the right side of the rear of the building, just past the sales and administrative offices, with the newspaper's mammoth and noisy presses, loading dock and distribution area centered at the rear of the building.

Newsroom computer networks were just beginning to emerge in the industry during that basketball season of 1979 and had yet to reach the newspaper. Here, journalism was practiced the old-school way. Typesetting was done on large and clunky Compugraphic machines, where the ladies in the composition room would physically enter copy submitted by reporters to have it regurgitated onto strips of white paper, where literally and figuratively, those strips would be cut and pasted. Not with the click of a computer mouse, but after being run through a hot wax machine and physically adhered to page templates. If there was a misspelling or editing needed, the ladies in the back room were experts with exacto blades and could correct a mistake or eliminate a paragraph to fit available space with the skill of heart surgeons.

Once each page was completed and proofed by department editors, they would sign off. The ready-to-roll pages would then be "shot," and thin replica plates of each page would be mounted and prepared for the day's press run. The deadline for the afternoon daily press run was a "hard" 4:40 p.m. When everything ran according to schedule, subscribers could expect their newspapers to hit distribution stands and driveways by early evening.

When the plates were all set, press manager Frank Voltoline, whose son played on the Seminole High football team, would hit the green power button. The presses would rumble to life and force the newsroom wall abutting the press room to shake violently like a spider on crack cocaine.

The newspaper during that 1979-80 basketball season was ram-rodded by managing editor Tom Giordano. A transplanted New Englander who retained his accent and slicked-back hair, Giordano supervised a small, but effective staff. He was old school and had developed his news story instincts about the community. Giordano could smell a story, large or small before the story knew it was a story.

He chain-smoked like a coal-fired energy plant, weaved his way around the newsroom like a nervous mother hen, and was responsible for the overall editorial content of the paper, and by extension, its page count, advertising success and penetration into the growing Seminole County market.

In his mid-40s at the time, Giordano's diminutive stature at 5'8" and weather-beaten face bellied his street fighter instincts. When he smelled a story, he refused to back off and would not be intimidated by the subjects of stories in progress especially if the subjects didn't necessarily want the stories to be published. He cowered to no one regardless of their position of power or authority and was a reliable two-fisted defender of his news and sports staff. Giordano's attitude was if a story affected the heart, health, or pocketbooks of readers, it was news.

In many respects, Giordano was a miniature version of actor Ed

Asner's gravelly voiced and gruff character "Lou Grant," a popular TV series that ran from 1977-1982. They both shared a penchant for rolled-up sleeves on their white shirts, raggedly affixed neckties, and a propensity to be a bit grumpy. In the course of a typical news day, Giordano would routinely work his way through a pack-and-a-half of Marlboros. Two packs if there were breaking stories hustled to bed against deadline pressure.

Sanford and Seminole County government coverage in 1979 was anchored by Donna Estes. With short-cropped salt-and-pepper hair and a no-nonsense attitude, Estes had developed a wealth of resources and contacts in the local government, business, and political communities around Seminole County. If it moved or breathed of a zoning issue, scandal, conflict of interest, or developing story with local political implications, Estes was on it. Like Giordano, she smoked like a fiend. She worked the phones, banged out her stories on a manual Underwood typewriter, and always got her sources to call back. They were almost as afraid to be left out of a story as included in a story.

Quiet and reserved Jane Casselberry handled features and obituaries, a delicate task within itself.

Doris Dietrich served as the "Lifestyles" editor for the newspaper. Focusing on weddings, engagements, and anniversaries, as well as the cultural and arts beats, she was the matron of the newsroom and the quintessential Southern Belle. During her more than 40 years at *The Sanford Herald*, she was always impeccably dressed, always with perfectly coiffed hair, and always with a faint scent of lavender perfume. Her beguiling hazel eyes, and sophisticated charm provided the perfect cover for a drop-dead sense of humor and a salty tongue when she was pissed.

Marva Hawkins served as the newspaper's connection to Sanford's sizeable Black community. Jovial and with an effervescent personality, if there was news to be derived from Sanford's black churches, businesses, cultural or educational scene, Marva was the first to know and the first to have it in print.

The staff was completed by news reporter Diane Petryk, a prissy, pain in the ass. An excellent writer, she took it upon herself to become the newsroom hall monitor and would chastise those who had burning cigarettes smoldering from desktop ashtrays while working on stories. She would frequently walk up to staffers who smoked and launch into thin-voiced tirades. The normal response from grizzled veterans like Estes was to simply smile, then blow smoke rings in her face. She would wheel in a huff, return to her desk, and the scenario would play out at least every other day.

Britt Smith sat in the copy editor's slot and reviewed news and sports copy submissions for grammar, spelling, and error-in-facts before edited story versions were sent to the ladies in composition.

If early October meant crunch time for a hectic sports schedule, it likewise marked a personal and professional milestone for me. On October 1, Giordano hired me to be the newspaper's new sports editor. At 25, I was a U.S. Army veteran and product of the military's Defense Information School at Ft. Benjamin Harrison, then located in Indianapolis. A graduate of both the Journalism and Broadcasting Schools there, I served time with Uncle Sam in Germany, first as a Public Information Specialist with the 1st Armored Division, and later as Senior Sports Announcer/Writer for the American Forces Radio and Television Network Headquarters-Europe in Frankfurt. Working at Armed Forces Network-Europe was certainly the highlight of my time spent in uniform and afforded me the opportunity to hone my sports writing and broadcasting skills. It also provided a dream experience of covering the 1976 Winter Olympics in nearby Innsbruck, Austria. By the time my enlistment was up, and I arrived in Seminole County, Florida in early 1977, I had enjoyed a fairly meteoric rise from my start in sports journalism as the 1973 Sports Editor of my high school newspaper, "The Roundtable," at Kellam High in Virginia Beach. Before coming to *The Sanford Herald* in 1979, I spent the previous two years as Sports Information Director for the Seminole Youth Sports Association, which ran one of the largest Pop Warner Football programs in the United States as well as other youth sports programs that included basketball, soccer, and golf throughout Seminole County.

It was through that position that I developed a solid grounding in the Seminole County sports landscape. As Sports Information Director for the youth organization, I had come to know and develop positive working relationships with the high school area athletic directors and many of the coaches, who readily shared their fields and courts, as well as their time and encouragement with the hundreds of youth volunteer sports coaches and thousands of young participants stretching across the entire county. The smart prep coaches frequently held clinics for each sport sharing their expertise. And the super smart prep coaches even shared their offensive and defensive schemes with their respective Pop Warner and youth basketball volunteer coaches.

It kind of stood to reason that if your eight-year-old Pee-Wee quarterback or point guard was familiar with the scheme of things they would see at the eventual high school level, they would arrive on a prep campus with half-a-dozen years of experience in executing those same offenses and defenses.

19

To this day, I'm convinced that the Seminole Youth Sports Association, under Director Don Ruedlinger, played a significant role in building and expanding both men's and women's sports at all levels around the county. And that would be borne out for years to come with the strengthening of every prep program in Seminole County north-to-south, east-to-west.

Just as Seminole County in 1979 stood in the shadows of burgeoning Orlando, *The Sanford Herald*, when it came to sports coverage, likewise stood in the shadows of the *Orlando Sentinel*, the dominant daily in the Central Florida region at the time.

During that period, the *Orlando Sentinel* was blessed with outstanding columnists like Larry Guest and Jerry Greene. The venerable Bill Buchalter was the Dean of prep sportswriters at the time and was a walking encyclopedia of high school teams, players, and results.

Like many large dailies, the *Orlando Sentinel* had mid-week and weekend regional tabloids that focused on county-by-county coverage around Seminole, Orange, Osceola, and Volusia counties. They were affectionately nicknamed, *"Little Sentinels."*

Veteran *Sentinel* sports scribe Herky Cush covered Seminole County and would become a friendly rival and sometimes golf partner of mine along with Lake Brantley coaches Bob Peterson and Gary Smith despite the competition between our two newspapers. For the record, Herky never beat me in golf.

What the *Orlando Sentinel* enjoyed in circulation advantage over *The Sanford Herald*, the *Herald* enjoyed in page count and column inches dedicated to Seminole County sports. And the distinct advantage was the *Herald* published daily except on Sunday, versus the *Sentinel's* twice-weekly publications. Cush had a larger audience, *The Sanford Herald* had the immediacy and frequency of a daily audience, and the luxury of more space, pages, and column inches dedicated to the Seminole County sports scene.

The Herald, at the time, was trying to grow its market penetration outside of Sanford and into other sections of Seminole County. Giordano was smart enough to understand that boosting sports coverage outside of Sanford alone, was a strategic way to build circulation and ad revenues. He gave me some budget flexibility to beef up what had largely, to that point, been a one-man sports department. While raises were rare, Giordano gave me an implicit "wink-wink" approval to fudge my monthly mileage reimbursement forms to throw a few extra dollars into my modest weekly paychecks. That seemed to work for our publisher Wayne Doyle as well since from an accounting standpoint, mileage was a "variable cost" and not a "fixed cost" when it came to crunching numbers. It worked for another reason as well. In short, the expanded sports coverage translated into additional advertising revenue and circulation growth for the newspaper.

Earlier in 1979, I met Sam Cook, an English and Journalism teacher at Lake Howell and Longwood Lyman. Cook was wired into Seminole County high school sports, and over cold beers and a shared interest in softball in the Casselberry Recreation League, we forged a personal and professional relationship. Cook, who would soon teach at Crooms Academy in Sanford, was brought on as a contributing sports columnist and sportswriter. Two years later, Cook would succeed me as sports editor of *The Sanford Herald* when I returned to my hometown of Erie, Pa., for an opportunity to work in minor league baseball as Public Relations Director and radio play-by-play voice of the Erie Cardinals, a Class-A affiliate of the St. Louis Cardinals, part of the New York-Penn League at the time.

It was through that friendship and Cook's connection to the high school journalism scene, that we developed a small cadre of budding sports journalists looking for their first bylines. Young guys like Benton Wood at Lyman High School, and Geoffrey Giordano, managing editor Tom Giordano's son, would join holdover sports stringer George Shriver in forming The Sanford Herald's young, but aggressive sports department.

If Santa Claus were ever to be reincarnated as a photographer, he would come back in the personage of the Herald's Tommy Vincent. Graced with a shockingly thick head of curly hair, and a beard that would make Rip Van Winkle envious, Vincent was the newspaper's chief photographer with as keen an eye for a great picture as piercing as his own steely baby blues. Vincent had been with the newspaper since dirt. At the writing of this book, he remains with the newspaper and probably will until the presses stop rolling. "Tommy V" was the master of the newspaper's photography staff when film at that time was still developed in dark rooms with red "safe" lights under deadline pressure. For decades, he had seen and photographed virtually every major newspaper story in Seminole County. Soft-spoken and with a wickedly dry sense of humor, if he ever gave up photography, he could easily find a budding career as a shopping mall Santa Claus; the physical resemblance was and remains stark.

Vincent was joined on the photography staff during Seminole High's 1979-80 run by veteran photographer Tom Netzel, a jack of all trades. Netzel could both shoot and write and would, on one day, have a photo and byline in the news section, the next in the sports section.

With no Internet or cell phones at the time, the sports staff would frequently type out their stories on paper, using manual type-writers, and employed a crude, but sophisticated method of filing stories to meet deadlines. It resembled a 1979 version of the Pony Express.

The Altamonte Springs Recreation Center was located dead center of Seminole County along the city line that separated the towns of Altamonte Springs and Longwood. Also known as Eastmonte, it was located along Magnolia Drive adjacent to a set of railroad tracks centrally located where most of the sports staff worked and lived. Unknown to Eddie Rose, Director of Eastmonte at the time, stringers like Benton Wood and others would return to their homes following mid-week game nights, type up their stories, and deposit them in the mailbox of the Eastmonte facility. Cook or I would swoop in during the wee hours of the morning, pick up the typed stories, review and edit them, then turn them over to Britt Smith and the composition department. This was certainly some violation of federal law concerning the unauthorized use of mailboxes, but our young and growing sports staff would rather beg for forgiveness than ask for permission. We were not above using guerrilla tactics in trying to beat the bigger *Orlando Sentinel* to the punch.

As October 1979 rolled out and November knocked on the door, late Friday nights in *The Sanford Herald* Sports Department resembled a finely choreographed dance. Our sportswriters would straggle in from their assigned games and locations, manual typewriters would clang loudly as we filed our stories. Pizza would be delivered, and Vincent and Netzel would work their magic in the darkroom and present proof sheets from which pictures of that night's games would be selected, sized, and cropped to accompany each game story.

By midnight on Fridays, the newsroom was abuzz in three-part harmony of putting stories to "bed." Our young sports scribes earned a whopping 20 cents a column inch—but more importantly, their first bylines. With our team in place, by October of 1979, the sports department buzz was reaching a crescendo.

Jerry Posey, who let Payne into the gym on Payne's first day that summer of 1977 at Seminole High, had rebounded his football team from a mid-season slump to earn a state playoff berth. The Lady Seminole's volleyball team would make a deep run into the state playoffs as well. Elsewhere around Seminole County, young coach Sammy Weir was reviving an underperforming football program at Lake Howell with the likes of Mike Wood and Bob Capobianco at quarterback and Division One prospect Bill Giovannetti at linebacker. Joe Montgomery had quietly built a juggernaut at 3A Oviedo High, with his Lions poised to make a deep playoff run, too. Former Penn State product Don Jonas would soon be named the first football coach at what was then Florida Tech which would blossom into the University of Central Florida.

As a high school kid, I'd actually seen Jonas play in the late 1960s as quarterback for the Norfolk Neptunes, a minor league team that played in ancient Foreman Field in Norfolk, just a few minutes from my high school stomping grounds in Va. Beach.

It was a heady time to be a member of *The Sanford Herald's* sports department. But even Jimmy the Greek could not have predicted the story that coach Bill Payne and his Sanford Seminoles basketball team would become and deliver in the winter of 1979.

CHAPTER 3
The Streak Begins

With pre-season drills, practices, and scrimmages complete, Seminole High's journey to the state basketball playoffs would begin in earnest the week of November 19.

A long-standing tradition, The Rotary Club of Seminole County South for the fifth year, would be sponsoring both a week-long basketball tournament, topped off by a high school football bowl game pitting a Five Star Conference entry against a Metro Conference team that week. Proceeds from the sports bonanza would benefit numerous charities around Seminole County.

The 1979 Rotary Bowl festivities would be a prelude to the hectic Thanksgiving week when some 5,000 Pop Warner football players, coaches, and families, from as far away as California, would descend on Seminole County and surrounding communities for a combination of youth football games, Central Florida attractions, and balmy weather, hosted by the *Seminole Youth Sports Association*.

With all of that going on as well as Seminole High and Oviedo High both embroiled in high school football playoffs, sleep would be a forgotten commodity for *The Sanford Herald* sports department that week.

Local hotels would be filled, restaurants would be swamped, and local attractions like Sea World and Disney would be strumming a steady beat through their turnstiles and piling up their cash registers receipts. Virtually every one of Seminole County's high school football fields would be booked solid with Pop Warner games scheduled from 8 a.m. and concluding with under the lights 8 p.m. kickoffs.

The entire sports week bonanza would be capped with a Friday night kickoff between Metro Conference football runners-up Edgewater, coming into the game with an 8-2 regular season record, pitted against the host Lyman Greyhounds, runners-up in the Five Star Conference at 6-4 to Jerry Posey's Seminole High gridders, who were advancing to the first round of Class 4-A football playoffs.

With the sports influx and activities stretching over the week, even the iconic and infamous landmarks like the topless strip joint Club Juana, the Fern Park Jai Alai Fronton at the intersection of Highways 17-92 and State Road 436 and the Sanford-Orlando Kennel Club off Dog Track Road would see a significant uptick in business. The entire week was made for a humorously alliterative headline of "Pigskins, Pasties, Pelotas, and Perfectas."

When we sat down for standard pre-season basketball interviews before the flurry of November sports activity, Seminole High coach Bill Payne spoke with surprising candor and confidence. While most coaches were somewhat guarded in their cautious optimism, Payne had a surprisingly positive perspective on how the season might play out.

During the week of the Rotary Bowl agenda, staff photographer Tom Netzel had just finished taking the customary team photos and individual player shots when Payne and I pulled up a seat along the wooden bleachers in the Seminole High gym to toss out questions and field answers on the '79-80 outlook.

"I'm kind of in a strange position," Payne told me.

"I've never been favored as a big winner until this year. It feels pretty good."

With four returning starters, a sixth man, and newly arrived Glenn Stambaugh penciled in on the roster, Payne didn't see the need to "Aw shucks," we might be OK with a few breaks," commentary.

The University of Tampa graduate, with previous prep coaching pitstops in Central Florida, including Colonial High, Ocoee High twice, and Watauga High in North Carolina, reflected on the team's progress since taking over the program in 1977.

"This is a team now," he told me.

"The racial garbage we had going on when I took over is gone now.

"These kids have really come together, and there's no doubt in my mind this is the best group of high school athletes I've ever coached."

Payne's pre-season comments went beyond the hardwood and the gym, derived from what he observed throughout the entire Sanford Community.

"It's tough to be a good high school athlete these days because there's so much more out there for kids to be involved and interested in. But credit our kids. They've put a lot of time and energy into making our sports programs good programs."

The third-year coach was also profuse in his praise of the entire Seminole High academic staff assisting a forward movement for the Tribe.

"One of our biggest assets here is Principal Don Reynolds, the staff, and the entire faculty," he commented.

"Everyone seems to be so involved, and the entire campus is just super to work with. That feeling rubs off on our athletes too."

With point-blank frankness, he told me, "You can look for Seminole High to become really good not just in basketball, but a lot of sports over the next five years."

And the veteran coach was wise to share the growing accolades and positive direction the Fighting Seminoles were earning where it counted significantly, on the domestic front.

"My wife, Barbara, and the kids (Billy, Lisa, and Susan) are really behind what we're doing. And that really helps.

"I guess you could say we're a 100-percent basketball family."

Payne's prophecy would prove to be accurate over the next five days of 1979 Rotary Bowl events. And well beyond. And his success during that 1979 season at Seminole High was a precursor to decades of winning seasons that would complete his coaching resume with tenures at nearby Seminole Community College, St. Petersburg Junior College on Florida's Gulf Coast, and Caldwell Community College and Technical Institute, nestled in the mountains of North Carolina where he would eventually retire.

The official beginning of Seminole High's record-breaking run would begin the evening of Monday, November 19. Payne's squad would face Bob Peterson's Lake Brantley Patriots in the opening game of the eight-team tournament with the nightcap game pitting the Leesburg Yellow Jackets from Lake County against the Deland Bulldogs from Volusia County.

Peterson's Patriots were the defending Rotary Bowl Champs from 1978 and were led by All-Conference guard Doug Dershimer. Unlike Seminole High, Peterson was not blessed with an abundance of basketball talent during that stretch at Lake Brantley. He was often tasked with coaching good all-around athletes and trying to convert them into exceptional basketball players. But make no mistake, Peterson could coach, and his teams were always tough and contributed to the dog-eat-dog competitive landscape of the Five Star Conference.

Second-round games of the eight-team draw Tuesday night would pit another pair of Five Star Conference entries against each other in an early season match-up when Greg Robinson's Lake Howell Silver Hawks, featuring sharp-shooting guard Bruce Brightman, against the always tough Lyman High Greyhounds, coached by Tom Lawrence. First-round action would be completed when the 3A Oviedo Lions from the nearby Orange Belt Conference tipped off against Orlando's Bishop Moore squad. It would be a testy opening act for Oviedo coach Dale "Digger" Phillips. Two of his starters would still be wearing shoulder pads as quarterback Troy Kessinger and running back Mike Scott were busily occupied helping football coach Joe Montgomery push on through two rounds of state football playoff action. A third starter, Horace Rolland would not make the season-opening lineup due to a sore knee.

But the Rotary Bowl Basketball Tournament would give Seminole County and Central Florida hoops fans their first look at the precocious freshman and man-child Ronnie Murphy. At 6-5 and a solid 225 pounds, Murphy would quickly become a dominant player in Central Florida and eventually go on to star at the University of Jacksonville. He would later be named the Sun Belt Conference Rookie of the Year and would also become the First-Round pick of the Portland Trailblazers in 1987.

Murphy had front-office issues over his playing weight, exacerbated by a serious foot injury that eventually led to a parting of ways with Portland following a settlement. He was out of the NBA after one year. In 1988 the Trailblazers released him following the suspension without pay twice for weight issues. Murphy would never again play in the NBA and tried a short-lived comeback in 1991 with the United States Basketball League.

It was no surprise that with the early season buzz of quality teams and the November thirst of local high school hoops fans, that the Lyman High gym was at capacity and packed early for the season-opening 7 p.m. tilt between Sanford and Lake Brantley. And fans got a tantalizing treat right out of the box.

In his final huddle before the first jump ball of the season, Payne gathered his squad and pumped them up with what would become a familiar pre-game battle cry.

"Play hard. Have fun."

The Seminoles did play hard. And as expected, so did Lake Brantley.

Bob Peterson's Patriots opened the game with a tenacious zone defense trying to mitigate Seminole High's height advantage and athleticism. Still, behind a balanced offense, Seminole edged out to a 19-12 advantage after the first quarter. Lake Brantley's Gary Hays came to play too, lighting up the second period with 11 points to help Lake Brantley close Seminole's lead to 34-30 at the half.

Two minutes into the third period, the Tribe's Bruce McCray would do what Bruce McCray would do at several points in that magical 1979 season. He took command of the game.

Seminole's senior forward, with the unusual array of inside shots, canned a dozen points in period three, then added a dozen more in the fourth period to go along with six, fourth-quarter rebounds and a pair of assists. Had it not been for the Patriot's All-Confer-ence guard Doug Dershimer returning fire with 14 of his 22 points in the final stanza, the score wouldn't have been as close as the final of 67-56 would indicate.

When the buzzer went off, Seminole was 1-0 in the young season. Payne wasn't at all surprised by Lake Brantley's competitiveness but was a little shocked at McCray's final numbers in the season opener.

"I'll tell you what," said Payne immediately after the game con-cluded.

"Lake Brantley is a lot better than many give them credit for. I thought we could have run a little bit more in the first half, but we had a terrible time attacking their zone. Believe me, we're happy for the win, and for the first game of the season, I thought both teams played well."

Patriot's coach Bob Peterson agreed and lamented a literal and figurative shortcoming his squad would face all season long: in-side size.

"I was pleased with some of the things we did tonight," said the defending Rotary Bowl Champions coach.

"We were in the ballgame until Seminole's size took control of the boards. There's just no substitute for the big men and we are not big."

As Payne headed for the locker room with victory number one in his back pocket, I asked him what he thought of McCray's game-high 32-points in a season opener.

"He had 32, really?"

"I knew Bruce got hot in the second half, but I didn't know he had that many. He's got a lot of different shots close in and when he's on, he is confident in his game."

With Seminole and Lake Brantley having set the table in the tournament opener, Orange Belt Conference entry Leesburg squared off against Five Star Conference member DeLand in the tournament's opening round nightcap.

The next afternoon's headline on Sports Page 1 read: "Tribe, 'Jackets Take Rotary Openers.

Sam Cook's game story profiled the Deland Bulldogs letting an 11-point lead escape their grasp as the Leesburg Yellow Jackets rallied in the fourth quarter for a 57-51 win. The game was won or lost if you will, at the foul line. The difference in the final score: Leesburg converted on 19 of 31 shots from the foul line while Deland would cash in on just 5 of 14 shots from the charity stripe. The loss would drop DeLand into a consolation game against Lake Brantley and would send Leesburg into a semi-final tournament showdown against Sanford's Seminoles.

The Rotary Bowl's second night of opening action featured four teams more than a little familiar with each other as Seminole, Orange, and Lake counties abutted each other like kissing cousins.

Sam Cook and young Benton Wood drew game assignments for Tuesday's completion of opening-round action in the basketball portion of Rotary Bowl week play.

Lyman and Lake Howell traded early first-half runs before Tom Lawrence's Greyhounds eased out to an eventual 66-58 win. Cook's story would profile great board work by Lyman's Kelvin Hillman who led the Lyman attack featuring double figure scoring from teammates Neal Gillis and Sam Lemon.

32

Lake Howell's Reggie Barnes was a one-man scoring machine for Greg Robinson's Silver Hawks in a losing effort, canning a game-high 25 points. At the close of the contest, Robinson lamented to Cook, "We got outrebounded 43-26 and committed 17 turnovers. That's not getting the job done."

In Tuesday's nightcap, Orlando Bishop Moore got double-figure scoring from the brothers Mullee—Greg with a game-high 21, Paul with 12, as well as double-figure scoring from Tim Koepsell with 15 and Greg Topper with 11 to manhandle the Oviedo Lions 84-52. Part of that lopsided score was attributed to Oviedo missing two starters still involved in football playoff games, a point not lost on winning coach Greg Robinson in his post-game comments to *Herald* sportswriter Benton Wood.

"Obviously Oviedo was at a disadvantage for the tournament with two of their starters still involved in football and a third down with an injury," commented Robinson.

Despite the lopsided margin, Oviedo coach Dale "Digger" Phillips did offer up a glimpse of a future star. Freshman Ronnie Murphy suited up and saw his first minutes as a varsity player, totaling nine points, five rebounds, and two blocked shots.

"As a true freshman, Ronnie has the potential to be a great one. But like a lot of young players, he still has a way to go," Oviedo's coach told Wood.

With the four opening round games completed, and losing teams bracketed for consolation day games, the tournament's semi-finals were set with Leesburg's Yellow Jackets squaring off against Sanford Seminole in Wednesday evening's opener and Lyman's Greyhounds facing Orlando Bishop Moore in the midweek nightcap.

Lyman's gym that Wednesday night was again packed, treating fans to a "Seminole County Takes on the World" feel to it. By night's end, it would be Seminole County 2, The World Zero.

Visiting Leesburg from neighboring Lake County tried to press Seminole early in the contest, but the guard tandem of Keith Whitney and Glen Stambaugh went to work like a pair of surgeons in the first semi-final of the night, slicing up the Yellow Jacket's press, leading to easy buckets. Sanford built an early 18-10 lead after one-quarter of play and never really looked back in cruising to an eventual 71-52 victory. Four starters hit double figures for Sanford which brought some post-game positives from Payne's early season perspective.

"We played loose tonight and had solid team defense," Payne told me after the win.

"I thought we handled their press well and got some three-on-two situations for some easy buckets. It was a solid defensive effort except when we fell asleep for a short stretch but got things back together."

Payne would stick around for the nightcap for some additional scouting in advance of Friday night's tournament championship game. And after witnessing Five Star Conference counterpart Lyman knock off Orlando Bishop Moore in the second semi-final game, he had a feeling of what his Sanford squad would likely see in the tournament title contest.

"Lyman looked tough tonight. I expect them to throw the press at us early and often come Friday night," he predicted to me.

Tom Lawrence's Greyhounds moved to 2-0 on the young season with a hard-fought 68-63 win over scrappy Bishop Moore. Senior Glen Bailey paced the Greyhounds with 24 points to lead four players in double figures. In a see-saw affair, Lyman used a 10-point run in the third quarter to squeeze out a back-and-forth lead over the Hornets.

Lawrence praised a solid team effort and singled out Bailey not only for his 24-point effort, but his defensive play matched up against Bishop Moore's leading scorer Greg Mullee. His post-game quotes to Benton Wood echoed Bailey's two-way performance.

"Bailey played a heck of a game tonight, including nine rebounds, and his defense held Mullee to six points," Lawrence told Wood in the post-game locker room.

"We got better in the second half tonight, and our bench helped out when we ran into some foul trouble. We pressed a lot in our opening game against Lake Howell, and I think that took something out of our legs early on."

Wood questioned Lawrence about the impending early season showdown against Sanford Seminole for the Rotary Bowl title.

"Seminole is big, and Seminole is quick," offered Lawrence.

"It's going to take a heck of an effort for our guys to beat them Friday night. Right now, we are happy to be 2-0 and hope we can carry this early season success into Friday night's game against Seminole."

With Sam Cook dispatched to one high school football playoff game and I dispatched to another, young *Sanford Herald* sportswriter Benton Wood drew the juicy assignment of covering Friday night's Rotary Bowl Basketball Championship game between backyard rivals Seminole and Lyman. Both the game and Wood's coverage lived up to expectations. Still a student at Lyman at the time, Wood had the biggest byline of his young career. His verbatim account:

A 21-4 fourth-quarter surge by the Sanford Seminoles gave them a come-from-behind 56-48 victory over Lyman in the finals of the Rotary Bowl Basketball Tournament.

In the consolation games, Oviedo edged Lake Brantley 65-61, Lake Howell eased by Five Star Conference foe DeLand 63-49 and Leesburg nipped Bishop Moore 59-58 in overtime.

"Lyman gave us a scare for 31 minutes," replied a jubilant Seminole coach Bill Payne after the victory.

That they did.

After the Seminoles jumped out to an 18-12 first quarter lead, the Greyhounds came charging back behind the play of junior forward Neal Gillis. He pumped in 12-first half points to give Lyman a slim 26-24 halftime lead.

"Losing Butler (Reggie) to foul trouble in the first half took away our inside game and hurt us tremendously," commented Payne.

Lyman opened up a seven-point lead at 38-31 with 1:39 remaining in the third period. They were led by senior guard Jeff Nelson who scored four clutch baskets for the Hounds in the third quarter as Lyman cruised to a 40-35 lead entering the fourth period.

After a basket by Gillis, the Seminoles went to work. Butler hit a layup to slice the Greyhound lead to 44-43 and former Lyman cager Glen Stambaugh came back to haunt his former teammates as he scored with 4:04 left in the game to give Seminole the lead for good 45-44.

The Tribe proceeded to up its lead as forward David Thomas hit a couple of buckets to expand the advantage to 56-44.

Lyman added two meaningless buckets to make the final score 56-48

Seminole was led by Bruce McCray who had 15 points, Thomas added 12 points while Stambaugh collected 11 for the Seminoles.

The Greyhounds were led by Gillis with 14 points, although he was shut down in the second half for only two points by the ferocious Seminole defense.

Nelson and guard Sam Lemon each chipped in with 12 points apiece for Lyman.

"Sanford Seminole has to be as good as anyone in the state," stated an amazed Lyman coach Tom Lawrence afterward.

"They have excellent personnel.

"Their size wore us down tonight. Bailey (Glen) got in foul trouble late in the game and it seemed everybody got hot all at once for Sanford."

Following the final whistle, Seminole High was quickly off to a 3-0 start and the Seminoles had some fresh hardware for the school's trophy case. There were center-court hugs from the team's cheerleaders, family, and friends as the Tribe gathered to raise their 1979 Rotary Bowl Trophy above their heads and pose for photos. And in the space of one week in that young basketball season, Sanford Seminole proved several points: They could play with a lead; they could come from behind; they could turn team defense up a notch when required, and they had developed early season poise.

And as the young basketball calendar continued to unfold in November of 1979, the prophetic observations of Lyman coach Tom Lawrence would be learned by others around Central Florida and beyond.

"Sanford Seminole has to be as good as anyone in the state."

CHAPTER 4

The Metro Comes Calling

With their newly minted Rotary Bowl Basketball hardware gleaming in the Seminole High trophy case, Bill Payne's team would have a week to prepare for their first regular season contest of 1979. And the first week of December would begin with a basketball bang rather than a whimper.

It seemed improbable just a trio of games into a new season that a high school basketball coach, or a coach at any level, would proclaim from the mountaintop, "This is the greatest game we've played since I've been here."

But that was Payne's post-game reaction to fellow *Sanford Herald* scribe Sam Cook when the Metro Conference's Boone Braves came knocking on Seminole's gym door the evening of December 1. And with good reason.

In the mid-to-late 1970s, the road to Florida's 4-A State Basketball Championship seemingly traveled through Orlando's Metro Conference I-4 corridor. Just a snapshot of how dominant Metro Conference teams were during that stretch:

In 1974, Metro Conference entry Winter Park lost the state title to a South Florida (Miami Jackson) team that was later declared ineligible.

In 1975, Metro Conference entry Maynard Evans won the state title behind Darryl Dawkins.

In 1976, Metro Conference entry Edgewater won the state title.

In 1977, it was Metro Conference entry Boone High's turn to claim the Class 4-A crown.

In 1978, Boone lost in the semi-final round of the State Class 4-A Tournament in Lakeland.

Tensions were high, tickets were scarce, and interest had skyrocketed when the Braves traveled to Seminole High that first Saturday night in December.

The teams did not face each other during the 1978 season, but in '77, when Payne's senior nucleus were budding sophomores, Boone saddled the Seminoles with a double-digit setback.

Although Payne wanted no chatter of "revenge," his feisty point guard Keith Whitney seemed more than willing following the Sanford team's terse, defensive battle that ended with the home team claiming a 48-39 victory to go 4-0 on the year, to at least discuss retribution and perhaps validation.

"It feels good," Whitney told Cook following the win.

"They whipped us by like 12 points in '77. We didn't play them in '78, so I wanted to whip them tonight."

In a see-saw affair that saw the Tribe wrestle control from the Braves in the third quarter, Seminole got balanced scoring from its starting five to build a 42-25 bulge at the end of three. Boone clawed back in the fourth to cut the final margin to nine points, mostly on some late driving baskets by Arthur Jackson and the fact Seminole went ice cold from the floor, not scoring at all in the last 5:07 of the game.

Payne had high praise for Jackson and even higher praise for his own mercurial point guard Whitney.

"Arthur Jackson is maybe the best player in the Metro Conference, and we did a pretty good job of holding him to 15 points," Payne commented afterward to Cook.

Sanford's Whitney would finish the Seminole win with a solid all-around game, totaling 13 points, handing out seven assists, and coming up with a pair of defensive steals. Forward David Thomas almost matched Whitney with 12 points, while Bruce McCray and Glenn Stambaugh each tossed in 10. Stambaugh was perfect from the charity stripe, harkening back to his free throw shooting skills honed while playing at Lyman before transferring to Seminole. In a free-throw marathon while at Lyman, he once had connected on 99 out of 100 foul shots.

"Keith Whitney has played games where he has done 100 things wrong," reflected Payne following the win.

"Tonight, he did 100 things right. This was the greatest game Keith Whitney has ever played."

Boone coach Wayne Rickman likewise came away impressed by Seminole High's win.

"It's tough to play catchup when you fall behind a good team," he told Cook.

"And Seminole is, sure enough, a top ten team in the state. They showed me something tonight."

More than 40 years after that 1979 win over Boone, Payne would reflect on what a key moment that victory was in a season that saw school record after school record fall by the wayside to his '79-80 squad.

"Looking back, that game was big for us. We came up huge. When you can not only play with the Metro teams but beat the Metro teams, that game was a real eye-opener for our kids. We came to play that night, and Whitney decided he was going to do things his way, and he did. Even early in the year, that Boone win was when we really started believing in ourselves as a team that we could beat anybody."

Over the next week-and-a-half, Payne's Seminoles did beat everybody and anybody. In impressive fashion. By mid-December, they were a perfect 7-0, following up their win over Boone with a trio of lopsided victories that included a 79-56 win over Payne's former team at Colonial High, another Metro Conference opponent; a 75-47 win over Five Star Conference rival Port Orange Spruce Creek, and a lopsided 88-58 win over Lake Brantley, a Five Star Conference neighbor they narrowly defeated in the opening round of November's Rotary Bowl Tournament.

Their unblemished record set the stage for an impending critical road contest against more muscle from the Metro Conference, the Maynard Evans Trojans.

With just a one-day turnaround between the lopsided win over Lake Brantley and the road clash against Evans, Payne's Seminoles would have only one practice session to prepare for the Metro Conference power on the road.

"They are just awfully hard to beat in their snake pit," Payne told me following the win over Lake Brantley's Patriots.

"They play that Triangle-Two and Box-and-One defense to perfection, and they are patient. We will have to play an excellent all-around ball game to beat the Trojans at their place."

As I made my way around the locker room for post-game comments after the win over Lake Brantley, Payne's undefeated disciples agreed the Evans Trojans would be a formidable litmus test.

"We'll have to keep our heads on," commented sharp-shooting guard Glen Stambaugh, feeling more comfortable in his role on the floor seven games into the season.

"We will have to play good defense and, of course, hit the foul shots," he predicted.

Forward Bruce McCray echoed the defensive mantra.

"Defense is the key, and we have to run—play our game," he offered.

Seminole High's soft-spoken big man in the middle, Reggie Butler, agreed with his teammates and coach.

While once reluctant to shoot, Butler too was growing more confident as an offensive option for the Seminoles but agreed the defensive side of the game plan would likely be the difference on the road and against Evans.

"When I have a shot, I'll take it," explained the senior center.

"But I worked hard on my defense all summer long, and my defense is paying off.

"The biggest thing I changed was bending my arm on blocking shots and slapping at the ball. I keep that arm straight now and it's much more effective."

***

Payne's description of the Evans High gymnasium as a "snake pit" might have been the basketball understatement of the year to that point.

Situated at the intersection of Silver Star Road and Pine Hills Road, the school first opened in 1958 and drew its initial student population from kids formerly bused to Edgewater High, Apopka High and, to some degree, Winter Park High.

The facility was named after local pharmacist Maynard Evans, who ran a downtown Orlando pharmacy and soda shop, "Evans Pharmacy."

The original construction did not include a gymnasium until the late 1960s when a gym, media center, and other expansions were added. For several years, Evans would share football facilities with Edgewater High at a nearby stadium known as the "Double-E."

Evans High was not fully integrated until 1971 and quickly became a dominating basketball powerhouse in Central Florida.

Back then, high school gymnasiums were indeed constructed like snake pits. The bleachers extended from opposite sideline walls almost onto the basketball courtside itself and placed fans within touching distance of both the home team and opposing team seating areas adjacent to the scorer's table.

Visiting teams at Evans were greeted by packed home crowds, raucous partisan cheering, and a smothering intensity that bordered on intimidation directed at opposing visitors who dared enter the Trojan's lair.

The walls were adorned with Conference Championship banners and other visual reminders of Evans' success in state basketball playoff action.

Both Payne and his coaching counterpart, Dick Hullette for Evans, could feel the unusual importance of a game this early in the season. And the emphasis on sticky defense and the likelihood of a low-scoring game soon played out. Cramped into the tiny scorer's table and sandwiched between the clock keeper and each team's statisticians, I watched the game unfold. Later that night, almost as physically, mentally, and psychologically exhausted as the players participating in the contest, I filed my story for the next day's Page 1

Sports Story with a 60-point Boudini-Bold headline screaming: **"Tribe Over Evans in Cat and Mouse Game."** The story in *The Sanford Herald* read:

For the better part of three quarters, Wednesday night, Seminole High and the Evans Trojans looked like they belonged in the Atlantic Coast Basketball Conference Tournament.

Seminole and Evans put on a classic display of stifling defense. Both squads showed remarkable patience. But with time running out midway through the final period, Seminole blew open a cagey cat-and-mouse game with eight unanswered points to beat Evans 43-36.

"We were scared to death," sighed a relieved Seminole coach, Bill Payne.

"You talk about basketball in Central Florida, you talk about Evans High," pointed out the Tribe's boss, whose squad upped its record to a perfect 8-0.

"Look at all the banners in this place. It's impressive. It's awesome."

Payne was referring to the numerous Metro Conference pennants gracing the Evans High gym walls, including the big green and yellow Trojan State Championship flag hanging above the visitor's first-half basket. Perhaps a visual reminder to intruders of the rich Trojan basketball legend.

Evans coach Dick Hullette had done his homework in preparation for the invading Seminoles. Choosing not to run and gun with the Tribe, the Trojans opened with a Kenny Grant basket a minute into the contest and then sat back and played a sticky zone defense, outrebounded the Tribe throughout the first half, and held on to the ball on a few occasions for as long as three minutes before

45

taking a shot by playing four-corners offense. Evans held the run-and-gun Seminoles in check, taking a first-period lead of 8-6 and stretching it to 14-9 seconds before halftime before Keith Whitney picked off a Trojans pass and raced for a Tribe layup to pull Seminole within three at intermission, 14-11.

"We didn't change anything at the half," pointed out Payne, who for the first time in his coaching career beat the Trojans in their own "snake pit."

"We just didn't get very many shots in the first half, hell, you can get a little cold when you only shoot once every four minutes."

Tribe guard Glenn Stambaugh opened things up a little by hitting three jumpers to go along with Reggie Butler's two inside buckets and Seminole took the lead for the first time in the game 25-24 at the end of three periods.

After three more minutes of cat and mouse, the Seminoles finally shook things up a little.

David Thomas, rebounding strongly in the second half, went back up with a pair of those rebounds for points.

Bruce McCray, held to four first-half points, connected on a pair of close-range shots and a pair of free throws before fouling out. Whitney canned a jumper and two more free throws and Stambaugh nailed his 15th and 16th straight foul shots of the season without a miss to push Seminole out in front to stay 40-30.

"That's all it took," commented Trojans coach Hullette.

"Just a short lapse and they had the game.

"Bill Payne has a good team. We put pressure on the ball all night and they handled it well.

"I have to say, though," added Hullette, "Our team has nothing to be ashamed of. We're young," he said, referring to the starting Trojan lineup featuring one sophomore and four juniors.

"My guys told me before the game, don't worry coach, we'll win," advised Payne following the contest.

"I'm pleased with our performance, we came back and beat them at their game," said Payne, whose only other coaching victory against Evans came back in 1974 in a home contest while coaching the Colonial High Grenadiers.

"I'll tell you what, I don't like this kind of basketball. I'm glad we don't play in the Metro Conference."

Payne might not have liked playing against teams in the Metro Conference prior to the 1979 season, but in '79-80, the Metro Conference teams would fall six times to his Seminoles, as the Tribe would go on to beat Evans on the road and at home, Boone on the road and at home, and Colonial on the road and at home.

Now 8-0, Payne's undefeated Seminoles were starting to kick up dust and began wondering when they might attract the attention of prep basketball pollsters around the state. But there was another storm brewing less than an hour away in Volusia County. Arch-rival Daytona Beach Mainland, under head coach Dick Toth, was matching Sanford High win-for-win and was likewise undefeated. And by a quirk of scheduling, Sanford's Seminoles and Daytona Beach Mainland's Buccaneers would not meet for the first of home-and-home games until following the Christmas break.

CHAPTER 5

Hey Pollsters, How 'Bout Some Respect?

With the traditional high school Christmas break right around the corner, Seminole's historic win over Evans on the night of December 12 would be part of a busy, three-game week for the Tribe. Next to come knocking on the door for the now 8-0 Seminoles, a very tall, and very talented Daytona Beach Seabreeze squad. The Sandcrabs would represent the first opponent thus far in the season, who could match and even exceed the Sanford team's height advantage along the front line of Reggie Butler, Bruce McCray, and the slinky David Thomas. The Sandcrabs also featured a pair of players who could play bombs away and shoot lights out from the parking lot.

And while Seabreeze had been receiving some early love from state-wide sports writers who voted to rank prep teams weekly, even at 8-0 and with a pair of early victories over traditional Metro powers Boone and Evans, there seemed to be no cracking the State's Top 20 Poll for Bill Payne's squad. That cold-shouldered neglect was beginning to be felt by some of the Sanford Seminoles who came into the Seabreeze contest with a little chip on their collective shoulders. And after the game, they weren't shy about expressing their unrequited basketball polling sentiments following win number nine, a solid 76-68 win over the Sandcrabs.

In a game not decided until mid-way through the final quarter, Seminole would again exhibit a final period will-to-win and take late control.

Payne was effusive in his praise for both teams and entirely satisfied with a three-win week in the books.

"They don't miss, do they?" declared Seminole's skipper in the locker room after the win.

Payne was referring to Seabreeze's talented guard tandem of Eric Ervin and Robert Robertson, who combined on outside shooting for 29 points to go along with a game-high 18 points from 6-9 center Rodney Williams. While Williams displayed a feather-soft touch from long range for a big man, he was forced to find shooting room on the outside perimeter, thanks to no less than six blocked shots in the first half alone by Seminole center Reggie Butler, who came up huge despite battling a flu bug.

The Tribe's starting five returned Seabreeze's fire from the opening tip.

Guard Keith Whitney nailed three early jumpers from the top of the key, backcourt mate Glenn Stambaugh hit nothing but net with a pair of long-range missiles from the right wing and forward Bruce McCray was seemingly impervious to Seabreeze's towering front line of 6-9, 6-7, 6-6. McCray, at 6-4, sliced and diced his way to seven inside points to help stake the Seminoles to a 20-19 lead at the close of the first quarter.

Playing taller than his 6-4 size, the Tribe's David Thomas took control of the boards, sweeping three consecutive defensive rebounds and shredding Seabreeze's press defense with a trio of laser passes to Stambaugh, who nailed three baseline bombs from 25 feet to push Sanford to a halftime lead of 39-34.

Then, a little strategy change for Payne and the Seminoles following intermission.

Saddled with three first-half fouls, Payne elected to sit his high-scoring forward McCray to start the third period and inserted steady backup Steve Grace into the lineup. He was immediately rewarded by the play of Grace, who would go on to earn an appointment to the U.S. Naval Academy following graduation. Grace gave Sanford four minutes of solid inside defense and picked up a couple of timely rebounds, saving McCray minutes on the bench.

"He did a really nice job when we needed it," Payne would later say of Grace's time on the floor.

With Grace providing shut-down defense, the first six minutes of period three belonged to the Seminole's Thomas. The lanky forward single-handedly took control of the boards on the way to a 12-rebound night, twisting underneath for a short jumper, connecting on a pair of foul shots, then turning the floor over to McCray--back in the game and off the bench. Seabreeze tightened the contest again as the third period continued to unfold with more outside shooting from guard Robert Robinson before McRay took matters into his own hands.

The well-rested senior quickly heated up, pouring in eight straight points, and punctuated the buzzer ending the third quarter with an electrifying dunk.

Still trailing Sanford, the Sandcrabs elected to shift to a full-court press as the final period got underway. The move backfired when the Tribe's lightning-quick Whitney hit the gas and climbed into the driver's seat of the Seminole offense.

Teaming with Stambaugh, the Seminole guards repeatedly trashed the full-court press, feeding their big men underneath for a series of easy buckets.

And at the game's end, Whitney made no bones about seizing

control of the contest.

"Ever since I've been here, I've been the only point guard. With Glenn out there to help beat the press, we can handle anybody. Seabreeze is good," added the senior playmaker. "But we aren't afraid of anybody."

As the fourth quarter unfolded, it was the Sanford team's turn to switch things up at the defensive end of the floor. The Tribe eschewed its usual man-to-man defense and dropped back into an improving sticky zone match-up.

"Give that credit to assistant coach Tom Smith," confessed Payne after the game.

"He kept telling me to go to a zone defense, and we finally did."

The calculated strategy switch pushed by Smith paid immediate dividends.

With Whitney and Stambaugh continuing to beat the Seabreeze pressure, Seminole put the game on ice. Big man Reggie Butler, who finished the night with eight blocked shots, shoved the game out of reach with a resounding slam dunk of his own to punctuate the 76-68 final score.

The soft-spoken Butler was a little more outspoken following his monster dunk.

"It felt good to ram it home," he smiled after the final buzzer.

"Hey, why not?"

"I had to match Bruce McCray's dunk, and I got a good pass from Glenn Stambaugh."

Thomas, who had a towering night on the boards, benefitted from steady feeds from Whitney and Stambaugh and had a robust offensive night, finishing with 17 points to go along with his dozen rebounds.

"Nobody can go one-on-one with him," Payne commented about Thomas' offensive outburst.

"They were spread out in that press, and David had a field day."

"We knew they were big, so we had to do something," the senior forward commented in the locker room.

"Last year, it was us who had to slow things down and try to press. Now, we can do things our way."

And Thomas tossed out a thinly veiled challenge to Florida Prep sportswriters who, thus far, had ignored his team's undefeated status and tough wins over Metro Conference competition.

"I hope this win gets us ranked. I think it should," closed out the Tribe's senior forward.

His comments were echoed by frontline mate Butler as well.

"We decided we have to do something to make people believe," said Butler.

"Maybe now they will."

Payne likewise joined the chorus of Sanford voices wondering what it would take for the Seminoles to get some respect from prep pollsters.

"The competition hasn't been bad this week, has it?" scoffed Payne.

The Seminole's coach was referring to Monday's 30-point win over Lake Brantley, Wednesday night's tough road victory against Metro Conference power Evans, and the just completed win over

Seabreeze.

"I think our performance this week should prove something to somebody.

"The win tonight combined with the win over Evans "AT" Evans has to say something for us," lobbied Payne.

Forty-eight hours after finishing off Daytona Beach Seabreeze to go 9-0 on the season, Payne and the Seminoles would get the validation they sought. In the weekly state rankings of prep basketball teams released on Tuesday, December 18, Sanford not only dented the state's Top 20, but the Tribe barged through the front door. Payne's Seminoles made their state-wide poll debut, creeping in with a number nine ranking in the state.

They would take that new-found lofty recognition into the opening round of the Oviedo-Outlook Christmas Invitational Tournament that tipped off Wednesday night, December 19. The venue was at Seminole Community College's gym, just a few miles down the road. The newly ranked Sanford team would respond with a record-breaking opening round win in the holiday event, and soon come to realize they were now walking around with a target on their backs. And Payne's early-season observation of Five Star Conference rivals would harken back to almost bite the Tribe in their collective basketball asses.

"Lake Brantley is a lot better than anybody gives them credit for."

■■

CHAPTER 6

The 12 Days of Christmas

The campus of Seminole Community College (SCC) was a six-mile hop, skip and southward jump down Highway 17-92 from *The Sanford Herald's* offices along the shores of Lake Monroe. It made for an easy commute for our sports staff covering the event leading up to the public-school system's Christmas break period.

The gymnasium on the rapidly expanding campus provided a larger seating venue than most high school gyms at the time and was the perfect central spot for Oviedo to play host to the Oviedo-Outlook Christmas Invitational. The gym was frequently referred to as the "House That Joe Built," in deference to Athletic Director and head basketball coach Joe Sterling.

The college, first established in 1965 and known then as Seminole Junior College, morphed into Seminole Community College in 1975 and became Seminole State College in 2009.

Sterling, one of the most respected coaches throughout Florida, was there from the beginning.

A two-sport star himself at Simon Kenton High in Independence, Kentucky, Sterling excelled in both basketball and baseball. At age 17, he enlisted in the U.S. Marines and would later go on to letter in both baseball and basketball at Auburn University following his military service.

Quiet, reserved, and disciplined, his coaching approach reflected his time spent in the military. His teams, both at the high school level and junior college levels, always played tough defense, had the patience to work for the best shot available, and win, lose or draw, did so with class and good sportsmanship.

Sterling found early coaching success at Greensboro High School in Florida's panhandle upon graduation from Auburn. He quickly built the program there and won a state title. He would move on to Apopka High just outside of Orlando and build a prep dynasty with the basketball Blue Darters, claiming a second Florida prep basketball championship.

When Seminole Junior College opened in 1965, he became Chair of the Physical Education Department, Athletic Director, and head basketball coach.

Under his direction, the Raider athletic department soon blossomed into a successful community college sports showcase, excelling in baseball, tennis, and basketball, where his teams were perennial 20-game winners.

Navy veteran John "Jack" Pantelias came aboard in 1973 as the college's head baseball coach. He would go on to win more than 650 games over 27 years and was perhaps one of the most colorful coaches I'd encountered in my sports writing career. He was a strict disciplinarian with a wicked sense of humor. Part Leo Durocher, part Don Rickles, and part Whitey Herzog, Pantelias was all business when it came to taking care of business on the diamond. And he could just as easily stop you in your tracks and have you rolling on the floor with one of his baseball idioms or sarcastically funny quotes that frequently rolled off his lips. Following his retirement in 2000, the baseball facility at Seminole State College would be renamed, "The Jack."

Head tennis coach Larry Castle likewise produced sterling results during that period with many of his teams and players advancing to national junior college championship play. And to help promote his sport, Castle contributed a regular tennis column to the sports pages of *The Sanford Herald*.

Sterling was an ambassador for the college and the community and never shied from helping promote sports throughout Seminole County and around the state.

He was also not shy about calling me from time to time with a recruiting request. Sunday was my only day off at the newspaper and on more than one Sunday occasion, I found myself sitting in Joe Sterling's kitchen, sharing a portfolio of newspaper clips designed to illustrate to prospective players just how much publicity and good ink the athletic programs generated from *The Sanford Herald*.

I'm not sure how much I helped him land potential recruits, but I do recall that Mrs. Sterling always served good food.

Bill Payne's success at Seminole High in 1979 likewise caught Sterling's attention. At the conclusion of that '79-80 season, Sterling would attempt to recruit all five of Seminole High's starters. And he met with some degree of success.

Sterling and Payne's basketball careers would become intertwined in 1982 when Sterling retired from coaching, stayed on as Athletic Director, and brought Payne aboard to succeed him as Seminole Community College's next head basketball coach.

Because school was already out for the Christmas break, the eight-team Oviedo-Outlook Christmas Invitational would feature both late afternoon and evening games. This meant our sports staff would pitch a tent in the college gym and make regular use of Joe Sterling's "hospitality room" adjacent to the entrance of the cavernous basketball court.

Between games, the press, officials, and visiting coaches were treated to a bevy of snacks, drinks, and the featured item throughout the event, Burger King Whoppers.

Manny Garcia Jr., in 1969 had purchased two Burger King stores and the franchise rights to several counties around the Orlando area. He was an avid supporter of youth and high school sports and helped establish the Burger King Player of the Week awards in Seminole County—dipping into his pockets to pay for the weekly plaques and end-of-season trophies. It was not at all unusual for football moms of *Seminole Youth Sports Association* Pop Warner football players to buzz by their neighborhood Burger Kings on the way to Saturday games to fill coolers with donated ice and orange drink to keep the little gridders hydrated, all on Garcia's dime.

I not sure how many Whoppers I downed during the week-long Oviedo-Outlook tournament, but to this day, I can't drive by a Burger King without reflecting on a great week of high school basketball.

And in the opening round of the tournament, Bill Payne's Sanford Seminoles delivered one whopper of a performance.

All five of Seminole County's high school teams would be in the tournament field along with Merritt Island from Brevard County, St. Cloud from Osceola County, and West Orange High from nearby Orlando.

And all five of Seminole County's teams arrived for the Christmas Invitational with varying degrees of success about one-third of the way through the season.

Wednesday night's opening games would feature the Lake Howell Silver Hawks matched up against West Orange. The two teams had met in the 1978 final of the Oviedo-Outlook Christmas Invitational, with the Orlando team knocking off the Silver Hawks.

Lake Howell coach Greg Robinson was looking more for consistency than revenge. He was working around an ankle injury to star guard Bruce Brightman, the emergence of Chuck Scott becoming a more regular fixture following the recently completed football season, and the steady play of veteran senior Reggie Barnes.

"Reggie Barnes is coming on like we know he can," said Robinson heading into the opener.

The second game of the night would feature Tom Lawrence's Lyman Greyhounds pitted against the host Oviedo Lions of coach Dale "Digger" Phillips. After a solid start to the season, Lyman had bogged down.

"We're just looking for a win right now," said Lawrence leading up to the game.

"We know Oviedo is better than when we beat them early in the season because of the starters they added when football was over. I think our kids realize that. This should be a tough game."

After a slow start, Phillips was now at full roster speed with the additions to his lineup of quarterback-turned-point guard Troy Kessinger, a now healthy forward in Horace Rolland, and the continued emergence of freshman Ronnie Murphy.

The second night of opening round action would showcase struggling Lake Brantley taking on St. Cloud. Lake Brantley would enter the contest winless on the season, the only team in the tournament without a marker in the "Win" column.

"We really don't know much about St. Cloud," commented Peterson leading up to Thursday night's first game.

"We tried to scout them, but they've been on the road a lot.

"We've come close a couple of times. We are improving on defense and have to take each game one at a time because of our lack of size. We have some hurdles to overcome and must be opportunistic."

The nightcap of the second round of opening games would see Bill Payne's undefeated Sanford squad squaring off against the Merritt Island Mustangs from neighboring Brevard County.

"I'm looking forward to an exciting tournament," was Payne's pregame assessment as he prepped his ninth-ranked team.

"There are some good teams involved, and we're just looking forward to playing our style of basketball. Nobody knows too much about Merritt Island so it's hard to comment on them."

With the stage set for the four-day event, it was time for the tournament's first jump ball.

Wednesday night's opener produced a tight game between Lake Howell and West Orange, and as *Sanford Herald* scribe Benton Wood wrote, Lake Howell coach Greg Robinson wasn't smiling about any aspect of the game.

In a rematch of last year's contest, the Lake Howell Silver Hawks avenged their defeat to the West Orange Warriors 52-48 in the opening round of the 1979 Oviedo-Outlook Christmas Invitational Wednesday night.

Silver Hawk coach Greg Robinson was less than pleased with his team's performance despite the victory.

"We stunk," he said flatly.

"We shot poorly, and we didn't concentrate on what we were doing on the floor."

Saying Lake Howell shot poorly was an understatement on Robinson's part. The Hawks were 7-37 from the floor in the first half.

Lake Howell and West Orange would play a back-and-forth contest for much of the game before Robinson inserted backup guard Mo Smith into the lineup, giving Lake Howell a defensive spark with three straight steals. From there, the Hawks got balanced scoring to squeeze out the win, but as he told Wood after the game, the victory was nothing to write home about.

"When you win a game playing as poorly as we did, you're awfully lucky," said Robinson.

"We are going to have to get more consistency out of some of our players to win our next game Friday night."

While Robinson was underwhelmed at his team's opening night win, Dale Phillips was pleased with a relatively easy victory over Lyman.

"It's nice to win the opener of your own tournament," he told me following the game.

With a deeper lineup this time around, Oviedo placed four players in double figures and blew open a close game at intermission by reeling off 12 unanswered points to begin the third period. From there, the Lions were able to rotate fresh legs throughout the second half and cruised to the 14-point win.

Lyman's Neal Gillis tried to keep the Greyhounds in the contest with an all-around solid game and 20 points, but his effort was offset by a game-high 24 points from Oviedo's Horace Rolland, a dozen by Troy Kessinger, 10 from Bill Burgess and a solid eight points from improving freshman Ronnie Murphy.

Oviedo's win was in stark contrast to the Lions' earlier season 13-

point loss to the Greyhounds, a fact not lost on Lyman coach Tom Lawrence.

"They outplayed us," Tom Lawrence told me after the game.

"We have some things to work on and straighten out."

Thursday night's second evening of opening-round games proved to be the best of times for Lake Brantley and the worst of times for visiting Merritt Island.

Sam Cook's story of the Lake Brantley-versus-St. Cloud game spoke for itself. Here's how he recounted the game that carried the headline **"Lake Brantley Defense Keys First Patriot Win."**

Break out the champagne.

Sound the trumpets and unleash the dancing girls.

After seven unsuccessful attempts, Lake Brantley finally tallied its first victory of the season Thursday night, 60-53 over St. Cloud in the Oviedo-Outlook Christmas Invitational.

The victory advances Bob Peterson's Patriots into an 8 p.m. semi-final Friday night.

The loss, St. Cloud's fourth against one win, relegates the Bulldogs to the consolation round Saturday afternoon.

"I hope this breaks the ice," a happy and relieved Peterson said about his initial victory.

"It breaks the tension. We won't be looking over our shoulders. Now we can play our game."

Cook would go on to recap in his game story that Lake Brantley got balanced scoring with Gary Hays totaling 14 points and All-

Conference guard Doug Dershimer adding 11, but it was a combination of continually shifting up the Patriot defenses and moving in and out of a four-corner offense that keyed the win.

If Peterson and the Patriots were no longer looking over their shoulder, the Merritt Island Mustangs were looking for the truck that rolled over them in the final opening round game against Seminole High.

Looking for its 10th straight win, the state's ninth-ranked Seminoles came out of the gate red hot, squirted out to an early 12-4 lead, and never looked back. Forwards David Thomas with 24 points and Bruce McCray with 28 would help Seminole build a 63-33 lead two minutes into the third period over the simply out-manned Mustangs.

Seminole coach Payne emptied his bench with a 30-point cushion when Merritt Island coach Haskell Light decided to go to a full-court press trying to drag his team back into the contest. Light quickly found that pressing the Seminoles wasn't exactly a sound strategy.

The Sanford team's backups, Steven Grace, Mike Gaudreau, Shun Thomas, and Clarence Sippio made the most of their playing minutes, shredding the Mustang press and helping build the final margin of victory to Seminole 97, Merritt Island 49.

The 97-point outburst by the Seminoles beat the single-game scoring record in the Oviedo-Outlook event previously held by Orlando Jones High set in 1977. Jones scored 91 in a winning effort against the host Lions that year.

Payne was sensitive to the final score and made a note of it in his post-game comments to me.

"No, we weren't trying to run up the score. They kept pressing and making mistakes and that led to us getting a lot of easy baskets.

I can't tell the guys on the bench not to score when they have layups for baskets," said Payne after the whopping win.

"We weren't trying to score 100 points either like the crowd was calling for.

"A lot of people didn't realize it but late in the game, we were closing in on the Seminole High record of 97 points. We tied it with reserves.

"I don't run up the score. I'm not that guy. I've had it done to me and I don't appreciate it.

With Thursday night's opening round completed, the tournament's semi-finals would be set for Friday with an all-Seminole County foursome. Host Oviedo would square off against Lake Howell in the evening's early game, while Seminole would face Lake Brantley for the third time just two months into the prep season.

In the space of 24 hours, Lake Howell coach Greg Robinson went from admonishing his team's poor opening-round play to handing out accolades for the Silver Hawks in the semi-final showdown with county rival Oviedo.

After a typically tight first half between the two teams, Silver Hawk senior Reggie Barnes and standout junior guard Bruce Brightman keyed a third period run by the Hawks with eight unanswered points to build a lead they would never relinquish en route to a 68-56 victory and a spot in the tournament's championship game.

Barnes would finish with 15 points and a dozen rebounds while Brightman connected for a game-high 22 points, contributing to Robinson singing a different post-game tune to Benton Wood.

"This was by far the best game we've played of the season," Robinson told Wood.

"We wanted to apply pressure on them because we knew coming in, they would be an improved team with players from the recent football season now on board."

Oviedo's Troy Kessinger led the host Lions with 16 points, but it was the double-double by freshman Ronnie Murphy that caught Robinson's accurate assessment of the emerging first-year player.

"He is going to be a great basketball player," raved Robinson of the opposing freshman.

"He really took control of the offensive boards, and he has a good outside shot."

Having pistol-whipped Lake Brantley by 30 points just a week prior, there was nothing much to suggest the Patriots would put up more than a nominal struggle against the talent-rich Seminole five in the nightcap semi-final.

But this was Five Star Conference basketball, and the old axiom that it's tough to beat the same team three times in one season came into play.

Bob Peterson elected not to try to run and gun with Bill Payne's Seminoles and played a game of drip-by-drip possession patience against the bigger and faster Sanford team. The strategy almost played out to perfection, and it wasn't until the final minute of the contest that Seminole High squeezed out a 45-42 win to preserve its undefeated status and move to 11-0 on the season.

Lake Brantley utilized the same strategy that led to their initial win of the season over St. Cloud. The Patriots frequently shifted defensive schemes and took the air out of the ball against Seminole with a four-corner offense that milked the clock and cut the game in half.

"We call it our four-for-the-score offense," explained the Patriot's Gary Hays.

"We work it, we work, it, we work it until somebody gets open for a layup."

Peterson further explained the strategy in our post-game interview.

"We knew we couldn't run with them, and we couldn't stay with them on the boards," enlightened the Lake Brantley skipper.

"We figured we would only get one shot when we had the ball, so we wanted it to be a high percentage shot."

While Payne's Seminoles were taken out of their up-tempo offense, it wasn't the first time that season they'd seen an opponent sit on the ball for minutes at a time. And they too displayed some first-half patience of their own.

Points were scarce to come by, but Seminole managed to edge out to a low scoring lead of 10-7 after one period of play.

Two minutes into the second frame, the Tribe's outside marksman Glenn Stambaugh connected on a pair of 20-foot jumpers, boosting Seminole to its largest lead of the first half 14-9, but Lake Brantley kept it close heading into intermission, trailing the Tribe by only six at 22-16.

Hays opened the third period with two quick buckets for Lake Brantley and Stambaugh answered with another outside bomb followed by a two-handed slam dunk from a frustrated Reggie

Butler to push Seminole's margin to seven points.

A fourth-quarter flurry led by Hays and Doug Dershimer tightened the contest to a three-point affair, and despite missing the front end of five straight one-and-one bonus shots from the foul line down the stretch, the Sanford team held off the Patriots for the 45-42 victory.

Seminole coach Payne was more relieved following the cat-and-mouse win than ecstatic.

"Lake Brantley really did a number on us tonight," sighed Payne in his post-game comments.

"They prepared well and really made us play their game."

Despite the loss and standing just 1-8 on the season, Peterson saw it as a pivotal moment for his Patriots.

"I think we grew up out there a little bit tonight," said the encouraged Lake Brantley coach.

"The kids played it tough all the way. I'm pleased, this was a good game for us."

Lake Howell's Greg Robinson stuck around for the semi-final nightcap to get a little more scouting in for his team's impending showdown with Seminole in Saturday night's championship game of the tournament, offering a candid assessment of his next challenge.

"That Sanford team has to be the best team I've seen in Seminole County since I've been coaching here," he offered.

"They are big, and they are quick, but we want to be in the big game—it should be a great basketball game."

With Christmas Eve knocking on the door, Seminole knocked out

Lake Howell that Saturday night, delivering the Tribe's 12th win on the season in a gift-wrapped 12-Days of Christmas victory before all the prep teams would take a week off for the holidays.

Bruce McCray and Keith Whitney keyed a fourth-period Seminole surge to break open a close contest and lead Sanford's squad to a 69-50 win, adding the Oviedo-Outlook Christmas Invitational Championship to Seminole High's growing list of credentials.

While Greg Robinson's Silver Hawks hung tough with the Tribe for three quarters, trailing just 41-38 heading into the final eight minutes, Seminole went to a stifling full-court press that resulted in a 13-2 run to ice the eventual 19-point victory.

"We were with them until the start of the fourth quarter," pointed out Robinson.

"They got a couple of quick baskets off the press, and we were forced to try to play their way."

And he added for the second time in 24 hours: *"Seminole is the best team I've seen in the time I've been coaching in Seminole County."*

Payne was both pleased with the win, and despite the growing number of victories and undefeated status, perhaps a little thankful for the impending holiday break.

"We haven't been doing our thing lately, and our thing is to run," he explained as the tournament teams were lining up for trophy presentations and the announcement of All-Tournament Player selections.

"Maybe the pressure of playing slowed-down and patient basketball is getting to our kids a little bit."

An appreciative crowd stuck around for the awards ceremony following the Tribe's 12th win of the year.

Despite the long days and late deadlines, one of the joys of covering tournaments like the Oviedo-Outlook Invitation was the reward of watching good basketball, and the honor of casting votes for All-Tournament Players.

To wrap up Saturday evening's festivities, I grabbed one more Burger King Whopper while casting my ballots as votes were counted up in Joe Sterling's Hospitality Room.

All-Tournament Selections for the event included:

Lake Howell: Bruce Brightman, Claude McKnight, Reggie Barnes.

Lake Brantley: Doug Dershimer.

Oviedo: Horace Rolland, Troy Kessinger.

Merritt Island: Carl Armstrong.

Lyman: Neal Gillis.

Sanford Seminole: David Thomas, Bruce McCray.

McCray, who led the Seminoles in scoring in 10 of their 12 wins on the season, was selected as the tournament's Most Valuable Player.

And as the curtain came down on the first half of the season, Payne sent his squad into the holidays with a message not necessarily about basketball.

"Take a break, get your mind off the game for a few days. Spend time with your family and friends and celebrate the meaning of the season," was his message.

And despite his suggestion, there was no doubt that Seminole

High would head into the holidays with one eye on the calendar that would soon unfold into a brand-new year. They would begin January knee-deep in District and Conference play. And the impending first showdown with equally undefeated Daytona Beach Mainland was drawing closer and closer. And the Buccaneers of coach Dick Toth had arrived at the Christmas break matching Seminole High victory for victory.

CHAPTER 7
Stretching the Streak

With the Christmas break concluded and the calendar flipped to the first week of 1980, Seminole High and the remainder of the Five Star Conference and District 9 teams would enter a steady stretch of facing familiar foes in testy conference matchups.

The second half of the season officially began for the Sanford Seminoles with a short trip down Highway 17-92 for a conference test against backyard rival Lyman on January 2. It would be the 13th game of the season for the Tribe, and they entered the un-friendly confines of the Greyhound's gym already with an eight-point and 11-point win over the 'Hounds.

Seminole began the new year with more a whimper than a bang, coming out of the holiday hiatus with no offensive rhythm and struggling to dispatch Lyman a third time. Seminole's eventual grind to a deceptive 60-49 win over Lyman, underscored a chink in his team's armor, prompting Payne to bemoan the Tribe's ef-forts and even question their number nine state ranking. At one point, the Seminoles were so out of sync, that Payne went to a four-corner offense, a ploy increasingly used by opposing coaches against the Tribe's preferred run-and-gun style of play. His post-game comments to Sam Cook illustrated his displeasure with his squad's efforts and perhaps prompted a little psychological ap-peal on the heels of his 13th win of the season.

"We're happy, aren't we?" Payne chided his squad in a morgue-like locker room after the win.

He propped himself up on two chairs and continued his post-game lament.

"We won. As long as we keep playing poorly and win basketball games, I'll be happy," he shook his head.

While Lyman chose not to run and gun with Seminole, the Greyhounds also elected not to go quietly into the night.

They didn't attack with a full-court press, but rolled out a very aggressive zone defense, stymying Seminole's leading scorer Bruce McCray through the first 16 minutes of play and forcing fellow forward David Thomas into early foul trouble. The net result was a chess match at the foul line that led to a slim 28-24 lead at the half.

"I guess I came out a little too aggressive," Thomas would relay to Cook in the post-game setting.

"The refs weren't letting us do too much out there tonight."

Fellow forward McCray shouldered some of the responsibility for a breakdown in the Seminole's offense with a candid confession to Cook.

"I've had some personal problems," admitted McCray about a lackluster first half.

"I just couldn't get my mind on the game."

Sanford came out in the third quarter still offensively flat, and the Tribe was clinging to a tenuous 42-36 lead after three periods of play.

And for the first time all season, Seminole's offensive woes prompted Payne to resort to an unusual game plan several teams had employed against him with increasing frequency 12 games into the season: a four-corners spread.

"We had to do something," an exasperated Payne said afterward.

71

"Nothing else had worked. We thought by going four-corners it might open things up in the middle a little bit."

The change in strategy worked, at least enough to allow Seminole to stretch its lead early in the fourth quarter and hold off any Lyman comeback threat.

Early in the fourth, David Thomas erupted for five unanswered points, McCray came out of his funk for a pair of buckets and reserve Shun Thomas aided the Seminole cause by connecting on six-of-six free throw attempts to push the Seminoles to the 11-point victory. It was at the foul line where much of the margin came for Seminole as the team hit on a total of 24 of 32 shots from the charity stripe, with Lyman connecting on 15 of 23 free throw attempts.

His Greyhound's effort against their county rival wasn't lost on Lyman coach Tom Lawrence, but neither was his frustration lessened at not being able to come up with a recipe to beat Seminole.

"They're a second shot team," pointed out Lawrence.

"They shoot it, and then they go get it."

The loss dropped Lyman to 6-6 on the season, leaving the Greyhound coach to contemplate the tough level of competition.

"We've lost six regular season games this year," he lamented.

"Two of them to Seminole and one of them to Daytona Beach Mainland, two of the best teams in the state."

While the loss left Lawrence scratching his head in search of an answer, the flat performance left Payne questioning just how good his 13-0 team was at that point in the season.

"We're not nearly as good as people think we are," an animated Payne commented to Cook.

"We might be the worst 13-0 team in the state."

Three nights later, Payne's players would show their coach that the Tribe's offensive woes were nothing more than just a passing fancy. Literally.

In game 14 of the year, the Seminoles broke out of their offensive malaise and shared the love, as well as the basketball. As a team, the Sanford squad dished out a season-high 20 assists en route to a comfortable 66-47 victory over the Silver Hawks.

After a tight first quarter, guards Glenn Stambaugh and lefty Keith Whitney began handing out assists inside like Christmas candy to forwards Bruce McCray and David Thomas, helping Payne's crew push their advantage to 41-23 at intermission.

Seminole came out for the third period ready to run, and their ability to find the open man helped the Tribe build an insurmountable lead.

"Sometimes we'd been guilty of overpassing," reflected Payne of the Seminole's frenzy of assists.

"But we try to emphasize getting the ball to the man closest to the basket."

Stambaugh combined with McCray and Thomas for five straight buckets to open the third frame, keyed by some crafty feeds by Whitney and it was off to the races for the Tribe. The offensive outburst was complimented by center Reggie Butler dominating the boards inside with a game-high 12 rebounds.

"Some people have been telling me I'm not playing up to my ability, but I knew I would jump well tonight if we could cut down on our turnovers," Butler commented about his defensive inside game against the Silver Hawks.

The 19-2 outburst allowed Payne to empty his bench halfway through the third quarter and for much of the remainder of the game, and he pointed to an additional wrinkle outside of the flurry of assists that seemed to have the Seminoles back to running on all eight cylinders.

"Maybe I'm getting smarter as the season goes on," Payne commented about his increased use and frequency of bringing reserve Shun Thomas off the bench earlier in games.

"Shun could be a starter on any other team in Seminole County."

But Payne's use of him off the bench suited the Seminole's sixth man role just fine.

"I like it like it is," Shun told Cook after the contest.

"I know that if Keith or Glenn get in trouble, I'll be in there."

Thomas also confirmed a players-only pre-game pow-wow took place ahead of the contest with the Silver Hawks, on the heels of the Tribe's abysmal performance against Lyman a few nights earlier.

His teammate David Thomas elaborated.

"We got together before the game tonight during sixth period," Thomas shared with Cook.

"I told my team, we've got to start playing like a ninth-ranked team again," said the Tribe's defensive enforcer.

Stambaugh added further confirmation of the players' internal conversation.

"Coach Payne told us in pre-game not to get down on ourselves, that we've got to play our game and not worry about what the other team is trying to do," said the sharp-shooting guard.

And Payne himself confirmed that the conversation among players only may have provided a much-needed pressure relief valve as Seminole High's win streak continued to build.

"I was really concerned coming into this game," Payne acknowledged to Cook in the post-game interview.

"I felt they may have been putting too much pressure on themselves and were expecting too much."

The season-high 20 assists and liberal use of his bench seemed to be the salve the Seminoles needed at 14-0 on the season.

Two days after their win over Lake Howell, Payne's ninth-ranked Sanford Seminoles made a big jump with pollsters.

On the heels of the Oviedo-Outlook Christmas Invitation wins, and a pair of victories to start 1980, state-wide sportswriters, who had once perhaps undervalued Sanford's start to the season, were now onboard the Seminole Express.

The January 7 Class 4-A Rankings moved Sanford's high school program from the ninth spot up to number five in the state. And they had company from Dick Toth's Daytona Beach Mainland Buccaneers. The Volusia County squad was likewise undefeated at 12-0 and sat in the number three spot in the poll. Two other teams that would come into play in Seminole High's future were also in the Top 10: West Palm Beach Twin Lakes held the number six spot while Tampa Robinson anchored the number eight spot in the poll.

One day after the poll was released, the Fighting Seminoles would take their elevated fifth spot ranking on the road to face Colonial High again. The Grenadier's campus and home court was a place familiar to Payne, having starred there during his prep playing days and eventually returning as coach before taking over the Sanford position. It was also the place where he met and eventually married his high school sweetheart, Barbara.

Win number 15 on the season for the Seminoles was almost single-handedly delivered by Sanford's big man in the middle, Reggie Butler.

Playing with growing confidence as the season wore on, the 6-6 center was a dominating force all night, blocking a total of 15 Colonial High shots to go along with forward Bruce McCray's game-high 24 points. The one-two punch contributed to the final score of Seminole 76, Colonial 59.

Colonial High coach Zeke Kenney had high praise for Seminole's man in the middle, who blocked the Grenadier's first five shots of the game.

"He's all-state without having to score a point," complimented Kenney of Butler's dominance in the paint.

"Without him in there, I think we could beat them."

Following his commanding defensive performance, Butler confided that he had received a little pre-game pep talk and motivation from his lighting quick point guard Keith Whitney.

"Keith and David (Thomas) told me not to let them come down the middle," confided Butler.

"I knew they would fake a shot, so I just kept my feet and waited."

While Butler's defensive prowess was impressive, so was Colonial High's one-three-one trap zone defense in the first quarter. With a warning from their coach about going back to a four-corners offense, Seminole found its footing in the second period behind the inside scoring of McCray and a stream of 20-foot jumpers by Stambaugh to slowly pull away and put the game in the hands of the team's reserves halfway through the third period to seal the victory and move the Sanford squad to 15-0 on the season.

As the season continued to unfold, and the Tribe's streak stretched on, the entire sports staff at *The Sanford Herald* wanted a piece of the coverage action. We jokingly did an office coin toss to determine who would cover the Seminoles in game 16 of the season. Young Benton Wood got lucky, won the coin toss, hopped in his car, and headed to the Seminole High campus with a little spring in his step and his lucky quarter in his pocket. There, the undefeated Seminoles would play host to the newest member of The Five Star Conference, the Apopka Blue Darters—the team Seminole Community College's Joe Sterling had taken to the state championship years earlier.

Seminole gave Wood plenty to write about.

Reggie Butler controlled the opening tip, Keith Whitney gathered it in and fed Glenn Stambaugh for a running layup five seconds into the game, and Sanford's team never looked back.

By the time 32 minutes of basketball had transpired, the Tribe had once again tied the school record for most points in a game for the second time in the season. They went on to rudely welcome their newest conference foe by walloping the host Blue Darters 97-60.

From the opening tip, the Seminoles were clicking both offensively and defensively, forcing eight Blue Darter turnovers in the first quarter alone.

"Anybody that tries to run with us is going to have a hard time," Payne understated to Wood after the game.

"The kids were psyched up tonight and we came ready to play."

On the way to the 97-point outburst, Seminole got one of its most balanced scoring nights of the season with David Thomas leading the way with 21 points, McCray with 18, Stambaugh with 16, and backcourt running mate Whitney with 13.

The Tribe's first-half performance meant plenty of minutes of playing time for the bench during the second half, earning compliments from their coach.

"Our reserves did a super job in the second half tonight. A lot of teams don't realize we have a solid bench.

"The trouble is, when you have 14 players on your team, you can't play them all at the same time," he told Wood.

Apopka coach Butch Helms came away impressed from his first-ever encounter against the home team.

"We were outclassed tonight," he told Wood after the defeat.

"But we'll play better against them the next time around."

Then Helms said out loud what most had been thinking with undefeated and third-ranked Daytona Beach Mainland less than a week away on Sanford's schedule.

"If Seminole plays like they did tonight, they'll beat Daytona Beach Mainland," predicted Helms.

When informed of Helms' comment, Payne had a quick response before Wood wrapped up his post-game interviews and tucked his reporter's notepad away.

"DeLand is our next game," snapped Payne.

"We will worry about Daytona Beach Mainland when the time

comes."

On Tuesday, January 15, Payne indeed had his squad focused on the next opponent just as the latest state-wide Class 4-A Poll was released. The rankings maintained both his team's number five spot in the poll and Daytona Beach Mainland's number three spot.

A record-breaking performance by Bruce McCray would guarantee win number 17 on the season and cement the impending showdown between two of the top five teams in the state, both undefeated.

Seminole opened game 17 with a smothering press against Art Parissi's DeLand Bulldogs, forcing four straight turnovers by Deland. A pair of blocked shots on DeLand's first two trips down the floor by Reggie Butler, combined with McCray's rocket scoring start put DeLand in an early hole.

The Bulldogs kept it respectable until halftime with some hot outside shooting, but McCray began the third quarter just as hot as he began the first, scoring early and scoring often. Butler kept the Bulldogs out of the paint with rebound-after-rebound on the night, and by the time McCray headed for the bench with 41 points to his credit, there were two minutes left in the game, and Sanford's native sons had put the contest out of reach.

Somehow, word quickly came down from the crowd that McCray was tied for the all-time single-game scoring record of 41 points held by former Seminoles Larry Kearse and John Zeuli.

Payne reinserted his senior forward back into the lineup hoping to give McCray a chance at the school record.

Smothered by a Bulldog press, McCray maneuvered himself to the foul line for a one-and-one opportunity with 16 seconds left in the game. With pin-drop silence in the gym, the senior forward knocked down both shots to erase the previous record with his 43-point performance and ice the Tribe's 77-65 win. While McCray was clearly the offensive story of the night, Reggie Butler was once again the defensive balance, providing the Seminoles with a total of seven blocked shots and a game-high 13 rebounds.

The victory set the stage for a showdown that had seemingly been building since the season's first tip-off: Seminole-versus-Daytona Beach Mainland. The drama was building as a pair of prep teams that had become the epicenter of high school basketball in Central Florida were about to face off in the first of two games against each other.

The only question that seemed to remain for the impending Friday night encounter that would take place in the Sanford team's home gym was, would the game live up to all the expectations and hype?

CHAPTER 8

Prelude to the Show Down

To characterize the entire city of Sanford as abuzz with anticipation of the impending Friday night match-up between Seminole High and Daytona Mainland would be a gross understatement. The event was ripe for sports writers to break out a virtual plethora of adjectives and a veritable cornucopia of adverbs to describe the impending game.

Downtown Sanford was on fire. Store-front signs of "Go Seminoles-Beat Buccaneers" popped up like garden weeds overnight. Breakfast chatter about the game that week began at the crack of dawn in the Colonial Room Restaurant and was the closing topic of conversation before the "last call for alcohol" at Wolfy's on Lake Monroe's waterfront.

There were decidedly shades of orange and black wardrobe attire around town reflecting Seminole High's school colors as both long-time fans and bandwagon newcomers showcased their support and interest in the game.

Demand for tickets prompted the school to set up two additional outlets to relieve pressure on the usual sole purchase spot at the school's bookstore.

Sweeney's Office Supply on Magnolia Avenue and Flagship Bank on Orlando Drive in Sanford would have tickets for sale on a first-come-first-served basis at the opening of business Wednesday morning January 16 for the Friday night contest. If you didn't have your tickets by noon that Wednesday, forget them. They were gone and you weren't getting into the gym.

Payne would huddle that week with his close circle of confidantes that included Jim "Doc" Terwilliger, the team's trainer, Dean Smith, team statistician, and tall and lanky Tom Smith, who would serve as the assistant coach that year. That trio was among the Seminole High group of people who befriended Payne upon his arrival at the school in 1977 and would play a part in the team's 1979 success.

Dean was a master at statistical information and worked up player tendencies, shooting habits, situational frequencies, and other tidbits of data that helped Sanford's coach in preparation for Mainland.

Visiting sports writers would often lean on him and pick his brain when preparing feature and preview pieces when teams came to play Seminole High.

Tom Smith (no relation to Dean) would also serve as junior varsity coach that year as well as varsity assistant coach and offer a calming counterbalance to Payne's fiery and enthusiastic approach to the game at the varsity level.

Terwilleger's roots were deep in Sanford and even deeper at Seminole High. His great-grandfather, Seth French, was one of the founders of the City of Sanford, and "Doc" was a graduate of Seminole High himself and played high school football there. Terwilleger would spend 37 years at the school, teaching in the Science Department. He would become Seminole County's first-ever Certified Athletic Trainer and played a significant role in helping establish Sports Medicine Programs at Seminole County's high schools.

The atmosphere on campus leading up to the game matched the electricity out in the Sanford Community. For weeks the team's cheerleaders had been making homemade basketball decorations that students, staff, and faculty would pin on their clothes in a show of support. Each week the decorations would change to reflect the winning streak. That week the theme of the decorations was "17-0."

Almost daily, assistant principal Wayne Epps, who would become principal at the school in 1981, would ride his motorcycle on campus, decked out in school colors with a mini banner urging the team on. Fellow coaches like Jerry Posey, assistant principal Lamar Richardson and a host of others offered encouragement and were wholly caught up in the excitement.

This would be no ordinary regular-season high school basketball game because this was no ordinary high school basketball situation. Rare was it when two teams arrived at a crossroads in the season both undefeated. Even rarer when they were from the same Conference and played in the same District. Still rarer when both were ranked among the state's top five teams in the largest school division.

And because the game provided a confluence of uniqueness, *The Sanford Herald* sports staff would give it the special attention it deserved.

Sam Cook began working on a pre-game feature piece on the contest that would focus on a survey of Seminole County and Volusia County coaches who had already played Seminole and Daytona Beach Mainland or would play both schools that season.

I got on the phone for pre-game interviews with both coaches and began a player-by-player profile and team match-up synopsis of the two squads.

Our combined stories consumed most of *The Sanford Herald's* sports pages published Thursday, January 17, the day before the showdown.

Sam might have had the tougher job. Most coaches are reluctant to divulge any comments that might lead to future locker room bulletin board material and give a team a psychological spark depending on what had been said.

But Sam had the uncanny ability to good-naturedly needle coaches and draw them out a bit. His pre-game feature did not disappoint. For some reason, the Volusia County coaches were more than happy to chip in with their predictions. Not so much for the Seminole County coaches.

Sam chuckled as he put the finishing touches on his story, sharing with me, "I've heard, hey, I still have to play these guys again more often than I heard the National Anthem this week."

His response to the coaches in our backyard: "Do you want to be the only Seminole County coach who doesn't make a prediction?"

Some shared excerpts from his coach's interviews that appeared in his *Sanford Herald* feature piece:

From Lake Howell's head coach Greg Robinson: *"Sanford's got two things going for them. Size (6-6 Reggie Butler and two 6-4s in Bruce McCray and David Thomas) and playing at home. Mainland's guards are better shooters, but I don't think they will shoot as well as they did against us (63 percent). My prediction—Sanford by two—in overtime."*

From Lake Brantley's head coach Bob Peterson: *"It will be one of the intangibles that wins it. Maybe the team that makes its free throws. Mainland relies on its running game, which is excellent, and Sanford uses a controlled fast break. It will be close. I wouldn't put a nickel on in."*

Cook had to poke Peterson one more time with, *"Do you want to be the only coach to not make a prediction?"* before Peterson laughingly coughed up, *"Seminole by one—in TRIPLE overtime."*

Lyman's head coach Tom Lawrence, who earlier had lamented that half his team's losses that season came at the hands of Seminole and Daytona Beach Mainland, added his prognostication.

"If it's a finesse game, Mainland will win. But if it's rough and physical, Seminole will beat them. Seminole is a second-shot team. They can go and get it on the boards. I'd like to see Seminole win, but I think it will be Mainland by six."

Both Volusia County coaches, which played near Daytona Beach Mainland's home turf, were a little more forthcoming and more decisive in their pre-game selections.

From Spruce Creek's head coach Joe Pigotte (who beat Mainland twice during the '78 season): *"Mainland has the best ball players and Sanford is more physical. I'll tell you how you beat Mainland. You can't let Sam Henry (Mainland's All-State guard candidate) handle the ball. He's the key to everything. My prediction, Mainland by 12."*

Deland's outspoken and colorful head coach Art Parissi weighed in with strong words as well.

"Mainland is the best team in the state. NOBODY can stay with them."

When Cook pointed out to Parissi that Lakeland High was currently ranked number one in the state compared to Mainland at number three and Seminole ranked fifth, he scoffed not once, but twice.

"Lakeland doesn't play ANY defense. Mainland has an excellent press and seven or eight players deep. Listen, Sanford doesn't have any guards (speaking directly about Seminole's backcourt of Keith

Whitney and Glenn Stambaugh). *The Mainland press will be too much for them the handle. My prediction, Mainland by 15."*

While Parissi's comments might have seemed a little bombastic, on closer pre-game analysis and in my pre-game interviews with both Seminole's Payne and Daytona Beach Mainland's first-year head coach Dick Toth, guard play emerged as what might be the deciding factor in the game.

Both teams arrived at this juncture in the season with perfect records. And despite their different styles of play, shared some striking similarities—two of the most significant among them: balanced scoring and pressure on the ball. And both had arrived at this point coming off impressive wins. Bruce McCray had just broken the single-game scoring record with 43 points against DeLand in that week's Tuesday night game while Daytona Beach Mainland thumped Lake Howell the same evening by scoring 100 points.

While McCray was typically the leading scorer for the Tribe, the remainder of the starting lineup offered a mix of balance and defense. Seventeen games into the season Seminole guards Keith Whitney and Glenn Stambaugh, along with forward David Thomas, were all averaging double figures to compliment McCray's team-leading average slightly south of 20-points per game. The only Seminole not in double figures was the Tribe's big man in the middle, Reggie Butler. Averaging seven offensive points per game, Butler made his living on defense, with an astounding seven blocked shots per game and an even dozen rebounds each contest.

The story was much the same for the Mainland Buccaneers, coming in at 16-0 on the year with an entire team core that had played together for the past eight years. While Payne took three seasons to build Sanford into a state contender, Mainland coach Dick Toth inherited a ready-made model. His starters had been together seemingly forever as part of the Daytona Beach Y.M.C.A. Youth Basketball Program and had moved right up the ladder together to the prep level.

Toth's squad likewise featured balanced scoring. Mainland's All-State guard candidate Sam Henry, whom DeLand coach Art Parissi had tabbed as the key to the game, entered the contest with a 17-point per game average while his 6-foot backcourt running mate Larry Prince was right behind at 14-points a contest. Although not the defensive force as Butler for the Seminoles, Buccaneer center Herb Harris matched the Tribe's big man in the middle at 6-6 and packed more offense at 16 points a game. Mainland's forwards, both at 6-3 were Jerry Smith with a 14-point average and Alvin Payne averaging 11.

On the eve of the contest, both coaches and players felt guards and the press could make the decisive difference in the outcome.

"We get good pressure on the ball," informed Toth, a basketball standout at the University of Georgia.

"That's why we score a lot, we get turnovers off the press and turn them into a lot of easy buckets."

While Seminole indeed pressed on the defensive side of the floor, the Tribe was more likely to run a variety of defensive schemes in the course of a game and ran a more "controlled" press.

"We've been able to get some easy scores off the press, too," agreed Payne.

Then he pointed out a team characteristic that some may have been overlooking.

"Everyone keeps saying that Bruce (McCray) shoots a lot and scores

a lot. That may be true because he's the outlet man off our press and gets a lot of shots close in."

To illustrate his point, Payne pointed out to me some of Dean Smith's statistics from the most recent game against DeLand in which McCray broke the single-game scoring record for Sanford High.

"Bruce scored 43 points, but did you see his shooting percentage?

"He hit 18 of 24 shots and only two of his shots came from farther out than six feet," Payne elaborated.

Even the high-scoring McCray himself downplayed his offense and felt the key to the game would be what Whitney and Stambaugh would be able to do against the Mainland defense.

"I don't care if I score but two points against Mainland," McCray told me following his 43-point performance against Deland.

"As long as we win the game, that's what counts. We know we have to break their press and control the ball."

The forward's senior guard tandem was in full agreement with McCray's observations.

"We have to be quick and make the good passes," offered the speedy southpaw Whitney.

"And not dribble the ball too much because they trap very well, especially off the in-bounds play."

Now fully solidified into the team's brotherhood as a Sanford Seminole starter, Stambaugh agreed.

"We know we have to beat their press, and equally important, we have to control the tempo of the game," the smooth-shooting senior told me.

"We have to play OUR game and our style to win."

Then both coaches put on their Public Relations and Chamber of Commerce hats as we were wrapping up the midweek phone interviews.

"You know, said Toth, *"if both teams play a good ball game, play up to their potential, it should be a great ball game.*

"I don't know if the fans realize it, but you have two pretty good ball teams less than 45 minutes from each other. That's unusual."

Sanford's Payne was in full agreement.

"It's nice that we have two teams from our conference ranked this year," he pointed out.

"The Five Star Conference has some good basketball these days."

Payne and his team would spend the two days leading up to the Mainland game focusing particularly on Mainland's starting five.

"All five of their starters can shoot," he offered in his preview of the contest.

"This game has been building for weeks, and it's hard for the kids on our team not to get keyed up. I don't want them to get too keyed up to where they can't go out and play once the game gets started. But I've never seen anything like this for a high school basketball game. The atmosphere on campus is like the NCAA Final Four," he admitted.

Payne's observations were perfectly illustrated early Friday afternoon, the day of the game. The Junior Varsity contest would start at 6:15 with the Varsity tilt between two of Central Florida's prep juggernauts scheduled for 8 p.m. But by mid-day Friday, the Seminole High parking lot was already beginning to fill with those lucky enough to have purchased tickets. And the closer it got to game time, the thicker the traffic around campus got and the more the electricity began to build in anticipation.

It was a short trip from the offices at *The Sanford Herald* to Seminole High for me that game night. And after finally finding a parking spot nearly a quarter mile from the gym, wielding my press badge, I got a friendly escort inside the already packed facility from two diligent Sanford Police Department officers on duty for the game. And I observed something I had never seen at a high school sporting event. There was such a demand for tickets, that ticket scalping was going on in the parking lot. I'm not sure how much some paid to get into the game, but it certainly left a mark on my memory banks.

"Wow," I quietly thought to myself. *"Ticket scalping at a regular season high school basketball game. This ought to be something special."*

CHAPTER 9

Sanford-Versus-Mainland: Round 1

Usually, when games of this magnitude play out, they conclude with one of three typical endings.

Outcome 1: Both teams show up and play a great game. Outcome 2: One team excels and the other bombs. Outcome 3: Somewhere in the middle.

After 32 minutes of basketball that Friday night, January 18, it took me forever to wrap up post-game interviews, fight my way through the throng at the gym and the overflowed parking lot at Seminole High, and shuttle my Plymouth Fury back to *The Sanford Herald* offices to file my story of "Undefeated Number Three-Versus-Undefeated Number Five."

We had deployed both of our ace photographers Tommy Vincent and Tom Netzel to shoot pictures that night because of the game's enormity. And as I sat in the corner of my newsroom sports cubicle near midnight, pounding out the game story on my manual Underwood, Vincent and Netzel were busy in the adjacent darkroom, conjuring up their combination of developer and fixer in plastic tubs of chemicals to bring their game photographs to life.

None of us spoke too much deep into the night except for exchanging, "great game, helluva game," while we practiced our crafts of writing and preparing pictures for the weekend edition of *The Sanford Herald.*

The easiest way to describe what happened between Sanford and Daytona Beach Mainland that Friday night is to simply share, verbatim, the game story I filed for the newspaper's next edition.

In bold, 72-point type, the story headline read: **Henry's Heroics Handle Seminoles 78-75**

All good things must come to an end.

Third-ranked Daytona Mainland ended the Sanford Seminoles 17 game winning streak Friday night before a frenzied packed house in a 78-75 thriller between two of the state's 4-A prep giants.

Mainland's All-State possible Sam Henry lifted the Buccaneers to the narrow, emotion-packed win with a season-high 32-point effort that proved to be the difference.

The contest was tied three times in the early stages with the Seminoles spurting to an 18-15 first-quarter lead behind six points by senior forward Bruce McCray.

A second-quarter surge, sparked by seven points from the sharp-shooting Henry, carried Mainland to a 38-32 halftime edge and set the stage for a heart-throbbing finish between the state's third and fifth-best prep teams.

Henry continued his torrid shooting from the floor to open the second half as he connected on 4-4 from the field on the way to a 14-of-23 performance that carried the Buccaneers to their biggest lead, 55-43 four minutes into the period.

"The turnovers and missed free throws in that spurt hurt is right there," pointed out Seminole coach Bill Payne.

"Mainland has the composure to do that, they've been to big games before and used it to their advantage."

The Tribe wasn't dead by a longshot, however.

Switching from an earlier game plan of trying to go inside to team scoring leader Bruce McCray, senior guard Glenn Stambaugh and backcourt mate Keith Whitney put up several outside jumpers to pull Seminole back into the contest.

Stambaugh canned 6-6 shots in the last eight minutes while Whitney and David Thomas hit a pair of jumpers each to pull Sanford within a single point with 12 seconds left in the game.

It was there that standouts Henry and David Thomas could have switched roles.

Thomas forced a Mainland turnover and fed a speeding Whitney who canned a 20-footer to pull Seminole within a single point 76-75.

The Bucs broke a frantic full-court Seminole press and seemingly had the contest in the bag when Henry earned a trip to the charity stripe on a foul by Thomas with seconds left.

The usually deadly shooter missed on the front end of a bonus situation, Thomas snagged the rebound and drove the length of the court but missed on a last-second opportunity to pull out a Seminole win when his intended pass to Bruce McCray sailed out of bounds.

Forced to foul with just three seconds left, Mainland converted from the foul line to put the finishing touches on a 78-75 victory.

"We would have liked to have had one more timeout there," said an exhausted Payne.

"David got the ball past half court with seven seconds, and we might have been able to set up a better shot."

But Payne would take nothing away from Mainland's showing.

"It was a super game between two super teams," offered Payne.

"We have to play them at least once more and hopefully twice."

Mainland coach Dick Toth echoed Payne's sentiments.

"They were really banging the boards," complimented Toth of Seminole's efforts.

"Our press helped us out a couple of times—it got us two or three quick steals that kept them from coming back."

Toth pointed out how he felt about the state rankings coming into the game.

"We try not to think about it.

"We're halfway there, and we've beaten every team. It was a good basketball game," added the former University of Georgia cager.

"There were a couple of points in the game where I was scared to death."

Surprisingly, Seminole had little trouble in cracking the Mainland press which had struck fear in the hearts of opponents.

"The turnovers were the difference," pointed out senior guard Keith Whitney.

"We broke their press without much of a problem, but we turned the ball over on our half of the court."

But the speedy point guard also took nothing away from the Buccaneers.

"They're a good basketball team, but we get another shot at them. They won on the road—so can we.

"We worked hard, really hard for this game. But we're going to start another winning streak and work until our tongues hang out."

The Tribe's leading scorer, McCray, felt a defensive change in the second half aided the Buccaneers.

"They started doubling up on me on and off," said the lanky senior who was held to five second-half points.

McCray, too, praised Henry's play.

"Sam played a ball game, he really did. Now we have to go back to work and try to beat them at their place."

Thomas, who ran into early foul trouble but came on in the second half, explained what he had in mind coming down the court with time running out.

"I was looking for Bruce sliding under the basket. He was there, but somebody had him blocked out. I don't think he saw the pass coming."

The Tribe's strong, silent leader, Reggie Butler, perhaps took the loss the hardest.

"I wanted this game," said the 6-6 center.

"Coach Payne told me I had to take the ball and go to the hoop more often."

Butler did just that, coming up with one of his finest all-around games of the year. The senior center tallied 14 points and crashed the boards for 16 rebounds.

"If things go right, we get them (Mainland) in the District Tournament. That's where it really counts," added Butler.

"They are a good basketball team," complimented Stambaugh.

"We started hitting some shots from the outside in the late stages of the game because they were sagging in the middle to keep us from going inside."

Stambaugh was one of the Tribe's main rally contributors with a game-high 20 points, 10 of them coming in the fourth quarter.

"That was a hell of a ball game," summed up Payne.

"If the people in Sanford aren't happy with our effort, I don't know what can make them happy.

"My guys played super. I'm proud of them. They've got nothing to be ashamed of."

So, two of the state's top five teams had clashed in a game that not only met expectations but also exceeded them. It was a game that left both teams physically, emotionally, psychologically, and mentally spent. And for the first time that season, Seminole High came up on the short end of the scoreboard, three points shy.

The regular season rematch between Seminole and Daytona Beach Mainland would come on the Buccaneers' home court. But not until more than a month later and ominously on the eve of the District 9 Tournament where teams would vie for a spot in Florida's 4-A State Basketball playoffs.

CHAPTER 10
Egos on the Rebound

While the Sanford Seminoles did their best to put on a false bravado in the post-game moments of the loss to Daytona Beach Mainland, Payne confided that his team was wounded, and he had little idea of how they would respond.

He got an inclination moments after the locker room cleared of the press and others, and the weight of the soul-crushing defeat settled in on players only.

"You mean after we got past the tears and the crying?" he confessed.

It was hard to put into context that critical moment in their season.

For two months, the winning streak had been building. For 17 games, they were challenged but unbeaten. They came from the point of no respect from state-wide pollsters to the lofty position of ranked fifth in the state. And the tension and stress that began to mount building up to the first encounter with the Buccaneers, boiled over in the gut-wrenching three-point loss on their home court.

Easily forgotten, perhaps, was the fact these were 17-and-18-year-old kids who carried into that game the weight of an undefeated season, the hopes of their entire school, and to some larger degree the well-wishes of the entire Sanford community and Seminole County.

"Look, going into that first game with Mainland, we were confident we were a good team. And we knew Mainland was a good basketball team.

"We knew their guards could shoot, but man, we didn't know the whole team could shoot like that," confided Payne.

Sanford center Reggie Butler was already looking a month ahead with his post-game comments including, "If things go right, we get them (Mainland) in the District Tournament. That's where it really counts."

Payne was more focused on the next regular season game and not what might be in store more than a month down the road.

"The Mainland game was a wake-up call. It gave our team a good dose of humility. Despite how good we thought we were, it showed our kids and me, that if we were going to be able to beat Mainland, things were going to have to be different. Something had to change, and we would have to find a way to get past them."

First, was the question, could the Seminoles pick themselves up off the psychological mat and prepare for their next regular season opponent? Payne was still searching for that answer four days following the loss to Mainland when familiar Five Star Conference foe Lake Brantley came calling for game number 18 of the season.

How the Seminoles would play was not the only question on the night of January 22. Also begging an answer was, which version of Bob Peterson's Lake Brantley Patriots would show up? The team that came within three points of beating Sanford in December's Oviedo-Outlook Christmas Invitational, or the same Lake Brantley team the Tribe had pounded by 30 points later in their first regular season encounter?

Adding uncertainty to the first post-Mainland game was the fact the already undersized Patriots would be without the services of All-Conference guard Doug Dershimer, who was sidelined with an ankle injury. More questions were posed when the Seminoles learned state pollsters had dropped them from their fifth spot ranking to eighth in the state following the Daytona Beach Mainland loss.

Payne would get his answer with some degree of certainty, but not a tremendous amount of conviction. His team methodically used its size advantage and outside shooting to carve out victory number 18, beating Lake Brantley to get back on track. At least on the surface, it appeared as if the Seminoles had put the loss to Mainland behind them.

The Tribe wrapped four three-point plays around hot shooting in the second and third quarters cruising to their 83-62 win over the Patriots.

Seminole incorporated a full-court press to open the game and behind the inside play of Reggie Butler and the outside bombs from guards Glenn Stambaugh and Keith Whitney, forged a first-quarter 18-10 lead.

Jeff McGarvey and Gary Hays tried to key a Lake Brantley comeback by combining for 16 points in the fourth quarter, but playing from behind, the Patriots were forced to press and foul. Seminole made its living at the free throw line in the final period, with 15 of the Tribe's 25 points coming at the charity stripe. Still, the Patriots had outscored Sanford 26-25 in the final stanza, a point not lost on Payne in the post-game discussion.

For the Patriots, staggering through a season with just one win to that point, it was a familiar refrain for head coach Bob Peterson. A good effort, but little in the way of wins.

"Jeff played a pretty good game tonight," complimented Peterson of McGarvey's 19-point, nine-rebound effort.

"He's been a little up and down this season, but he seems to play well against Seminole."

Payne too was handing out post-game accolades, this time to his bench which got significant minutes thanks to Sanford's hot start and consistent lead.

The Tribe's coach was especially complimentary of reserve center Steve Grace's effort against Lake Brantley.

"We're trying to get him more playing time," Payne explained.

"We have to have another big man we can turn to with confidence in crucial situations."

Grace earned the compliments with solid defense, a good job on the boards, and by contributing with nine points offensively while spelling starter Reggie Butler in the paint.

Despite the fact the Patriots entered the game with just one win against 15 losses, Payne was wary of a potential hangover from the Mainland loss the previous Friday night.

"I was concerned about how we would play tonight and telling you the truth, throw won loss records out the window when you play conference opponents.

"I really wasn't expecting a good game from our kids tonight."

His point guard corroborated the Sanford coach's concern,

"Before the game, everybody seemed a little flat," shared Keith Whitney.

"So, we kicked coach out of the locker room for a few minutes and got ourselves pumped up."

Patriots coach Bob Peterson pointed to two separate benchmarks in the game that he felt made the difference in the outcome.

"I think our kids missed the presence of our senior leader, Doug Dershimer, at the start tonight, and of course, then they got hot in the third period, too," offered Peterson.

And the Patriot's skipper returned to a theme that had plagued his squad all season—lack of height.

"We just couldn't contend with McCray, Butler, and Thomas inside," Peterson said of Seminole's front line. "If our center (Jeff Sevor) had three more inches, he'd be the best center around here."

Despite standing only 6-1, Sevor indeed had a solid inside game against the Seminoles, finishing the night with 14 points. But it was hardly enough to offset double-digit scoring by the Tribe's McCray, Stambaugh, Butler, and Whitney, all retiring to the bench one minute into the fourth quarter, allowing Payne's reserves to register significant minutes of game time.

The road wouldn't get any softer for either squad as conference play would continue with Friday night matchups set for January 25. Seminole would look for win number 19 on the season by hitting the road to take on Spruce Creek. At the same time, Lake Brantley faced the unenviable task of meeting the conference's only remaining undefeated team, Daytona Beach Mainland.

CHAPTER 11
Billboard Material and the Braves

To this day, nobody on the Seminole High basketball team will either confirm or deny, that comments made previously by Spruce Creek head coach Joe Piggote, had anything to do with the Friday night beat down Sanford administered to the Hawks in their gym on January 25. Maybe the hosting Hawks had an inkling it was coming as a paltry 200 showed up to witness the game.

After all, it was Piggote, who had boldly claimed in Sam Cook's preview story 10 days previous, that Mainland would not only beat Sanford in the clash of undefeated teams but also beat them soundly by 12. The Seminoles might have also hung a clip of DeLand's coach Art Parrisi's comments on the locker room bulletin board for additional motivation.

"My prediction, Mainland by 15. Sanford doesn't have any guards," stated Parrisi.

It was highly unusual that an opposing coach would single out two players by name—namely guards Glenn Stambaugh and Keith Whitney, as weak links in a lineup. And who could blame Sanford if they used those coaches' comments for some personal motivation and inspiration?

That appeared to be the case as Seminole High's guards sparked some torrid shooting from the floor, led a smothering press, and punched Piggote's Spruce Creek team in the nose for their 19th win of the season.

Shooting at 63-percent field goal accuracy from the floor, the Tribe literally beat up Spruce Creek and took the Hawk's lunch money. Final score: Sanford 73, Spruce Creek 47.

A glance into team statistician Dean Smith's numbers indicated just how thoroughly Sanford controlled the game in virtually every aspect.

Those questionable Sanford guards? After center Reggie Butler slammed home a vicious dunk to get the party started just eight seconds into the game, Whitney and Stambaugh took control. In just over two- quarters of play, Sanford's left-handed spark plug was a perfect four-for-four from the floor and carved up the Spruce Creek defense with laser precision, chalking up 11 assists. Stambaugh quickly notched 14 points with his patented 25-foot jump shot from the right side of the key before calling it an early night and hitting the bench.

When Sanford's guards weren't driving Piggote nuts, the Seminole's big men inside were. Leading scorer Bruce McCray was off to the races with 17 points, Butler added a dozen and David Thomas was a one-man rebounding machine, pushing Sanford to a dominating 41-15 halftime lead. For all intents and purposes, the game was over at that point.

"This was probably as good a first half as we've played all season.

"First of all, our big guys psyched them out, then we controlled the boards, and then we got red hot," observed Payne.

"I have to say that Keith (Whitney) probably had his best all-around game of the year tonight, too."

And Payne was quick to praise the overall defensive effort when his Seminoles were not shooting at a torrid pace.

"Our defense was super as well. We jumped on them early and never really let up. It was a pleasant game to coach," he understated.

Then the Sanford coach turned his attention to the next two games on the Tribe's schedule.

"Next week looks like bad news, really bad news," he predicted.

"We've got Boone and Daytona Seabreeze coming up and both of those are on the road."

Payne's recollection of his team's earlier season 48-39 win over Metro power Boone on Seminole's home court, was still fresh. And despite his team easily handling Seabreeze in their first encounter, offered a scouting glance at what he expected in the next two games.

Regardless of being 3-0 against Metro teams at that point in the season, Payne was taking nothing for granted.

"Boone has won something like nine straight games," pointed out Payne.

"When you do that in the Metro Conference, you have to be playing some good basketball. And Seabreeze has been playing a lot better lately. Their big kids are young, but they are playing with a lot more confidence as the season goes on," he offered.

One final takeaway from the convincing win over Spruce Creek was borne out in Dean Smith's magical book of numbers and statistics. By hitting 63 percent field goal accuracy against the Hawks, number crunching revealed that Sanford's starting five had shot at least 50 percent from the floor in every game on the way to a 19-1 season log. In short, that shooting percentage would be tested with a road trip to Orlando, where the Tribe would be facing a hostile home crowd and a Braves team looking to exact some revenge for their earlier season loss to Sanford.

Even at the high school level, there is something ethereal about a 20-win season. And as Payne prepped his squad for its Wednesday, January 30 encounter against the Boone Braves, it would be that other-worldly benchmark of 20 victories that Sanford would be shooting for.

The game would be a match-up between the Metro Conference's first-place team and the Five Star Conference's second-place team.

Sanford would step into the Braves gym, ranking as the eighth-best team in the state. But there would be plenty of noise to greet the Seminoles.

"Those crowds are fanatical in the Metro Conference," Payne said in advance.

"I went over to scout Boone the other night and I made the mistake of wearing a Seminole jacket into the game. I heard plenty from the fans," he admitted half-jokingly.

Along with the crowd noise, his team would also have to deal once again with the slow, deliberate pace most Metro teams preferred to play. It would be a clash of styles for his run-and-gun Seminoles.

"Boone is like most teams in the Metro. They play that slow-tempo, controlled game. Against West Orange the other night Boone held the ball for the entire third quarter. That can drive you nuts," provided Payne in a mini-scouting report.

And while his Tribe would have to again deal with the not-so-subtle style of a four-corners offense certain to be utilized by the Braves, there were discernable changes taking place within Sanford's chemistry and statistics. Those nuances signified a slight shift in team balance since the streak-stopping loss to Daytona Beach Mainland.

Soft-spoken center Reggie Butler was scoring more, and leading scorer Bruce McCray was rebounding more.

"I was looking into recent statistics going into the game tonight with Boone," explained Sanford coach Payne.

"Reggie has 182 rebounds on the season and Bruce now has 181. Reggie's been going to the hole a little more often with the ball and that's helped a lot."

Payne's assessment was accurate. Heading into the Boone game, Butler, who averaged a little over 7 points a game in the first half of the season to go along with a dozen rebounds and six blocked shots per contest, was now routinely scoring 12-14 points a night and had connected on his last six straight shots from the field.

Along with more offensive balance and more equitable rebounding, Sanford was enjoying some new-found respect from the Orlando media market as well. Maybe because it was Orlando-Boone next up on the schedule, but TV stations had come out to do pregame features on the Tribe leading up to the Wednesday night tilt.

Sanford had indeed dropped from fifth to eighth in state rankings following the loss to Daytona Beach Mainland but had since won two impressive games and two teams ahead of them in the state poll had suffered defeats but remained locked in their ranked positions.

"Two teams in front of us both lost and stayed right where they were at. It would seem reasonable we would move up a notch," lobbied the Sanford coach.

Young Benton Wood won another coin toss and drew the Boone-

Sanford game assignment. His short and sweet story lead in Thursday afternoon's *Sanford Herald* removed the suspense about the game's outcome:

Twenty and 1.

Bill Payne's Fighting Seminoles reached that magic plateau Wednesday night as they struggled to a 50-44 win over Metro Conference leader Boone.

Sanford is now just a game shy of tying the school's single-season all-time win record of 21.

Bruce McCray turned in a stellar performance, scoring 23 points and pulling down nine rebounds. Thirteen of those points came in the final 11 minutes of the ball game as the Seminoles turned a 22-20 third-quarter deficit into a 14-point lead late in the ball game.

Neither team got off to a fast start, neither owned more than a four-point lead in the first half and as the half came to a close the two squads were deadlocked at 20-20.

Boone's Tony Oliver opened the third period with a layup to give the Braves a two-point lead, but Reggie Butler quickly followed with his lone basket of the evening, and David Thomas connected on a free throw, giving the Seminoles the lead for good 23-22.

Keith Whitney and Bruce McCray tallied six points apiece in the remainder of the quarter to give Sanford a comfortable 35-28 lead as they entered the final eight minutes.

The Seminoles continued to build their lead in the final stanza.

With 1:37 showing on the clock, the Tribe owned a 46-32 advantage, but the Braves battled back as they ran off nine straight points, closing the margin to 48-44 with five seconds left in the game.

Boone's senior forward Matt Butler stood at the foul line with a chance to slice the Sanford lead to two points, but he missed the front end of a one-and-one situation. McCray was fouled as he grabbed the rebound and calmly sank both free throws to put the finishing touches on the Seminole's 20th victory of the season.

"They were fundamentally ready for us," observed coach Bill Payne.

"We didn't match up with them well. They forced us into a few turn-overs which hurt us at the end."

Sanford held the Brave's scoring leader Arthur Jackson to only 12 points. The talented senior guard entered the contest with a bet-ter than 17-point average, second-best in the Metro Conference.

"We went with the zone defense late in the second quarter," con-tinued Payne.

"We stuck with it in the second half, and they got cold from the outside."

The loss marked the second time this season that Boone has been turned back by the Seminoles.

Sanford won the first meeting 48-39.

The Braves remain 7-0 in Metro Conference play.

The loss marked the first time they've been beaten at home this season.

The Seminoles will take their show on the road Friday night as they tangle with Five Star Conference foe Daytona Beach Seabreeze.

"Seabreeze always gives us a big game at their place," remarked Payne.

"We've lost the last two or three ball games when we've been

over there."

The win over Boone accomplished both a team goal and an individual mark for Payne.

The 50-44 victory helped the Seminoles reach the Holy Basketball Grail of a 20-win season and served as some personal redemption for Payne. Having struggled for Metro Conference wins as Colonial High's coach prior to coming to Sanford, Payne was now a perfect 5-0 against Metro Conference competition. There would be one more Metro Conference encounter on the Tribe's schedule when the Evans Trojans would travel to Sanford for a rematch. Evans would be seeking revenge for Sanford's 43-36 win earlier in the season in another testy chess match between slow-tempo and run-and-gun play styles.

CHAPTER 12

Fit To Be Tied and Front-Page Stuff

As the first week of February unfolded, it appeared as if Bill Payne's Sanford Seminoles had righted their ship and managed to put the sting of a 17-game streak-ending loss to Daytona Beach Mainland firmly in the rear-view mirror. But plenty of work remained leading up to the all-important District 9 Tournament.

That work began on Friday night, February 1st, and began on the road, where to this point in the season, Sanford had proven itself to be road worthy. At 20-1, the Tribe had not lost a game playing on an opponent's home court, including three tough road wins against the talented Metro Conference.

That accomplishment remained intact as they took their show on the road and rode a big inside game from center Reggie Butler and forward Bruce McCray, along with the perfect free-throw shooting of marksman Glenn Stambaugh to knock off Daytona Seabreeze 61-49. The win marked the 21st of the season for the Tribe and tied the school's all-time single season win record. One of the few Five Star Conference teams that matched up size-wise with Sanford, the front line of Butler, McCray, and rebounding machine David Thomas shut down the Sandcrabs front line of 6-7, 6-6, and 6-6, holding that trio to just 14 points in the paint.

Butler, playing with more offensive confidence, chalked up 14 inside points himself which combined with McCray's 21, was more than enough to offset a solid effort by Seabreeze's slick junior Rodney Williams, who pumped in a game-high 23.

"Yeah, but those were all from the outside," Payne pointed out of Sanford's dominance under the boards.

110

For three quarters, Sanford owned the paint with McCray and Butler jerking down nine rebounds apiece and helping Sanford build a comfortable lead heading into the final period. Trailing and forced to press and foul, Seabreeze made the fatal mistake of sending Sanford's charity stripe assassin, Glenn Stambaugh, to the free-throw line. The sharp-shooting senior, who entered the game with 90-percent free throw accuracy, sank seven straight foul shots to put the game on ice in the final stanza.

While Sanford was busy canning 23-30 free throws on the night, Seabreeze was almost as cold as the Seminoles were hot. The Sandcrabs cashed in on a mere 5-14 opportunities from the foul line as the Seminoles pulled away.

Payne was quick to praise his big men for their yeoman's work against Seabreeze's front line.

"Reggie had a super effort tonight," complimented Payne.

"He and Bruce did an excellent job of controlling their big men.

"It was pretty rough out there tonight. I thought the kids did a good job of handling themselves in a somewhat hostile environment."

The Sanford coach was also happy for the show of support as plenty of Seminole high faithful made the 40-mile-plus trip and turned up in the stands to witness the team's record-tying victory.

"I'm glad to see a lot of our people made the trip to see us play over here," he smiled.

"Having our folks in the stands helped a lot."

With a record-breaking opportunity now presenting itself with one more win on the season, Payne was quick to dispatch any thoughts of the Seminoles getting ahead of themselves.

"We've got Lyman coming to our place next and they're always ready for us. The team has been working hard and they don't want to get beat by anybody the rest of the way."

The Sanford skipper also squashed any thoughts of his team peaking as they were coming down the home stretch of a historic regular season.

"I'm not one to believe in peaking," responded the Seminole coach.

"All I know is right now, we're playing good basketball, and we want to continue to play good basketball going into the District Tournament at the end of the month.

"You really don't know what it's like to peak until you're on your way down. And the way the kids have been playing, I don't think we're on our way down."

After filing my story on the win over Seabreeze and on the way out of the office for a short weekend break, managing editor Tom Giordano flagged me down and called me into his office.

In between a mushroom cloud of smoke from his ever-present pack of Marlboro's, he wanted to double-check on a few things.

"So, this coming Tuesday night against Lyman, Sanford High can break the school record for regular season wins?" he asked.

"That's where we stand," I confirmed.

"They tied the school record at 21 wins with the victory over Seabreeze. Lyman always plays Seminole tough, but this one is in Sanford's gym, so they have home-court advantage."

Giordano soaked in my response, took another drag on his cigarette then smiled and leaned over his desk.

"Joseph, no pressure but bring your writing "A-Game" Tuesday night. If Sanford breaks the school record, we're moving the story from the sports page and on to Page 1, above the fold," he chuckled.

I left his office pumped. Page 1 is nirvana for any journalist worth his salt. And Page 1 above the fold is where the eagles fly. As much as I was looking forward to the weekend, I couldn't wait for the Tuesday night match-up between the Tribe and Tom Lawrence's pesky Greyhounds.

In the blink of an eye, the short weekend had come and gone and as I was prepping my pre-game story the morning of Tuesday, February 5th, the new Class 4-A State High School Basketball rankings were released. Following their three-point loss to Daytona Beach Mainland, pollsters had dropped the Seminoles from 5th to 8th in state rankings. And after four straight wins following that 78-75 loss to the rival Buccaneers, Sanford High was once again getting some love from across the state. Heading into that night's 8 p.m. tipoff against the Lyman Greyhounds, Sanford had moved back up in the poll from 8th to 5th, and Daytona Beach Mainland had also been bumped up to second in the state behind Lakeland. The new poll would add a little more spice to the backyard brawl between the Seminoles and the visiting Greyhounds in a game Bill Payne was approaching with cautious optimism. That old sports axiom of "it's hard to beat the same team three times in one season" crept into pre-game thoughts.

"Lyman has always played us tough," commented Payne in our Tuesday morning phone interview.

"We had a couple of hard games against them earlier in the season and we know they'd like nothing better than to come in here and knock us off."

Payne's concern was certainly justified. Tom Lawrence's *Greyhounds* had played like that little girl with the curl from a nursery rhyme the entire season. When they were good, they were very, very good, capable of beating most other teams in the Five Star Conference. And a good deal of those from surrounding Central Florida regions. But when they were bad, not so much.

The question was, which Greyhound team would show up at 8 p.m.?

By 9:30 that night, Payne's Sanford Seminoles broke the school single-season victory record, all questions were answered about which Greyhound team would show up, and I had my Page 1, above-the-fold story in print.

Tuesday night's Five Star Conference clash between the Fighting Seminoles and Lyman Greyhounds was one for the record books...the Seminole High School all-time single season record books, that is.

Bill Payne's run-and-gun squad shook off some early first-quarter lethargy, dominated the boards, and exploded in the third quarter to whip the Greyhounds 79-57.

The victory marked the 22nd of the season for the Seminoles, re-writing the all-time single-season mark set nine years ago by coach Joe Mills and his Larry Pearce and Billy Corso-led squad that notched 21 wins before losing to Martin County in the regional round of state playoff action.

While the Seminoles rewrote the record book, they also put some nice touches on the 22nd winning chapter of the season in typical

114

Tribe fashion: a four-act play.

It was Tom Lawrence's Greyhounds who owned the first half of chapter one, however.

Quick buckets by Greyhounds Sam Lemon and Kelvin Hillman pushed Lyman to a fast 4-0 lead, prompting Payne to signal for an equally fast timeout.

The early Seminole rest brought less than fruitful results however as Lemon canned another jumper and forward Neal Gillis hit his second bucket to push Lyman to an 8-0 lead four minutes into the game.

It was there that Payne signaled for the full-court press which brought about immediate results.

"We had to do something," pointed out Payne about the change in strategy.

"They had us on the ropes early."

Seminole, in the form of senior forward Bruce McCray, bounced off the ropes and back into the contest quickly.

McCray hit two fast hoops, added a slicing tip-in, then got help from a David Thomas eight-foot shot and a 20-footer from Glenn Stambaugh. By the end of the first stanza, the Tribe had a 16-12 lead which they never relinquished.

"They started hitting the boards and controlling things," allowed Greyhound boss Tom Lawrence.

"That kind of threw us out of whack and off our game plan."

Big men Reggie Butler, McCray, and Thomas also threw the Greyhounds off their shooting plan. With the three lanky seniors dominating on the inside, the Greyhounds went frigid from the floor, connecting on just one of 13 shots from the field in the second period.

Lyman salvaged some grace, however, by hitting 11-12 free throws in the period to stay within striking distance. The Greyhound's journey to the charity stripe also spelled early foul trouble for two Seminole starters, Stambaugh and McCray.

Stambaugh picked up his third personal foul at 4:22 in the second quarter and McCray picked up his third a minute later. But super-subs Shun Thomas and Stephen Grace came off the bench and picked up the Tribe offense to lift Seminole to a 33-25 halftime lead.

"Shun and Stephen really did a good job coming in like that when we needed them," complimented Payne of his reserves.

"Our starters get most of the publicity, but we have a lot of good ball players on this team."

Thomas and Grace then accounted for 10 of the Tribe's 20 third-quarter points to build the margin to 45-31 with 3:37 remaining in the period.

Enter Mr. McCray once more. The senior forward made his presence known immediately by cruising inside for three fast buckets that sealed Lyman's doom.

McCray finished the evening by once again leading the Tribe efforts with 24 points to go along with his eight rebounds. Seminole placed four starters in double figures in the record-breaking win. Backcourt aces Stambaugh and Keith Whitney chipped in with 10 points each while senior center Reggie Butler tallied a dozen points to go along with 12 rebounds. Forward David Thomas hit six points down the stretch but enjoyed his best night on the boards this season by nailing 15 rebounds.

"Coach Payne told us to start crashing the boards and to make something happen," the slender senior pointed out.

"We did and we got out ahead of them. It feels good to break the school winning record."

"Coach Payne told us point blank we better start crashing the boards, echoed Butler, the Tribe's 6-6 enforcer.

"We all feel good about breaking the school record. We want to finish with four more wins to build our own record now."

Neal Gillis and Sam Lemon paved the Lyman effort with 11 and 10 points respectively in the loss that dropped the Greyhounds to 10-11.

To put a time-stamp perspective on where the Seminoles stood with that record-breaking 22nd win, a scramble for school record book information revealed several marks already broken to that point, and several more that were well within reach with four games remaining in the regular season. A statistical snapshot of that moment in time revealed:

*This team twice tied the school record with the most points in a single game with 97. The school record was set in 1959 and tied again in 1977.

*With Tuesday night's record-breaking 22nd win of the season, the front line of forwards Bruce McCray and David Thomas, along with center Reggie Butler, combined to set a new single-game rebounding record with a total of 51. The previous record of 45 was set during the 1972 season.

*With 22 wins out of 23 games to this point, the Seminoles were fast closing in on the best school won-loss record in school history of 21-7, set in 1972.

*Through 23 games, this crop of Seminoles was averaging 70 points per game, well ahead of the school record of 67.7 points per game set in 1968.

*The school's all-time single-season field goal percentage record was well within reach. Payne's '79-'80 team stood at averaging 57 percent from the field following the win over Lyman, with the old-school record of 54 percent set in 1970.

*Scoring leader Bruce McCray had broken the single-game points record with 43 earlier in the season against DeLand, breaking the record previously shared by Larry Kearse in 1970 and John Zeuli in 1974.

*It was in that game against DeLand that McCray also broke the school record for most individual field goals in a game with 18, breaking the previous record of 17 by Ruben Cotton, who at that moment was starring for the University of Central Florida basketball squad just miles away from Sanford.

*Shooting guard Glenn Stambaugh was making a serious run at the school record for free throw percentage for the season. The record at that moment in time was 80 percent for the year set by John Zeuli during the 1974 season and tied at 80 percent a year later by Randy Brown. Following the February 5th rout over the Greyhounds, Stambaugh was shooting a torrid 94 percent from the charity stripe, and it seemed he would either have to break an arm or miss the team bus for the next four games not to set a new school record.

And no one knew as the Seminoles stood at 22-1, just how critical Stambaugh's accuracy from the free throw line would become. Or when exactly it would come into play, but it would.

CHAPTER 13
Nail-Biters and Blowouts

Seminole High would look to pad its new school record for single-season victories in the next week with a February 8th game on the road against Five Star Conference rival Lake Howell and a rematch against Metro Conference power Orlando Evans on the Tribe's home court on February 12th. Neither game would be a piece of cake.

Seminole had dispatched coach Greg Robinson's Lake Howell Silver Hawks 69-50 much earlier in the season, but that was then, and this was now. Evans would again present the same problem all Metro Conference teams presented: a slow, deliberate style of play, and frequently holding the ball in a four-corners offense.

Tribe coach Bill Payne was a seasoned enough coach not to look past Lake Howell with an eye on finishing the year undefeated against the Orlando Metro Conference, and with good reason.

Off to a slow start, Lake Howell had improved steadily over the season. And although Robinson's squad would host Seminole High with an even 10-10 record on the year, the Silver Hawks had been soaring of late, coming into the contest with three wins in the past 10 days.

Payne's consternation about the road game against his cross-county rival was justified. His team was lucky to escape the Lake Howell gym with its modest five-game win streak and lofty state ranking intact. My game story Saturday morning in *The Sanford Herald* was a description of how to "win ugly."

It wasn't pretty, but it was exciting. It wasn't artistic, but it was close. It wasn't a masterpiece, but it was a victory.

Lake Howell's much improved Silver Hawks came close, very close, to knocking off Bill Payne's fifth-ranked Fighting Seminoles Friday night in a Five Star Conference battle. But a big third-quarter cushion enabled the 23-1 Tribe to hang on for a 74-68 win and escape with its record and state ranking untarnished.

"They do that to us every time we play them, they get sky high every time they play us," said a sweat-soaked, relieved, and some-what unsatisfied Seminole coach Bill Payne afterward.

"I would have to say this was the worst team effort we've had all year. We had a lot of people doing a lot of things wrong out there tonight."

While the Seminoles were doing things wrong, Greg Robinson's Hawks were doing just about everything right in the first half. The teams were knotted at 18-all after a sizzling first quarter.

Tribe guard Glenn Stambaugh and forward Bruce McCray carried the weight for Seminole in period number one with six points each while sizzling rival Reggie Barnes pumped in 10 first period points in a one-man shooting exhibition to answer for Lake Howell.

The Seminoles and the Silver Hawks maintained the close battle through the first four minutes of the second period before a pair of jumpers by senior Lake Howell forward Claude McKnight pushed the Silver Hawk's lead to 28-24.

Payne called for the patented Tribe full-court press once again, and once again it proved effective.

David Thomas made good on two trips to the charity stripe, Stam-baugh canned a jumper and added another free throw and Shun Thomas converted on two foul shots as the Seminoles found them-

selves back on top 30-28 with a minute and a half remaining before intermission.

The Seminoles stretched their lead to 34-30 and headed for the locker room for a rest as Reggie Butler smashed a Bruce Brightman shot into the stands to end the first-half battle.

Typically, the third quarter belonged to Seminole, and the surge after halftime provided the winning cushion and victory-saving margin.

Electing not to run and gun with the Tribe as he had done in the first half, coach Greg Robinson called on his Silver Hawks to slow the pace and change the strategy.

"Sure, we ran with them in the first half," explained Robinson.

"But we're not a run-and-gun team. We had to slow things down a little."

While the Hawks were slowing down Bruce McCray was picking up steam after hitting the bench early with three first-half personals. The senior forward pumped in 12 points in the third period to offset eight by Lake Howell's Reggie Barnes to help the Tribe outscore the Silver Hawks 24-19 in the third stanza.

McCray kept up his hot hand in the first three minutes of the fourth period with three more inside hoops to help Seminole build a 16-point lead before Lake Howell came roaring back into the contest.

The Silver Hawks applied a full-court press of their own, coming up with five steals. Larry Mincey canned a trio of long jumpers from the top of the key and Lake Howell found itself right back in the thick of things, cutting an 11-point lead to six with a minute to go.

Seminole traded last-minute hoops with the Hawks to maintain the edge and preserve the six-point win.

"We've been playing with more intensity lately," Robinson complimented on his squad's effort.

"But we could have done a little better job with our zone defense. We got hurt by their big men on the baseline while we were in our zone."

"We certainly didn't look like the number five team tonight," observed Payne after the contest.

"But don't take anything away at all from Lake Howell. They always give us fits. I just hope we don't have to play them in the District Tournament."

While Payne never liked to look ahead. He may well have peered into a crystal ball following the escape from the Silver Hawk gym. As the regular season played out, and seedings were beginning to take shape for the upcoming District 9 Tournament, Sanford and Lake Howell would indeed clash again.

With win number 23 secured, the Tribe would return to the friendly confines of the Seminole High gym to host Orlando Evans. The Trojans and the Seminoles would meet in the rematch exactly two months to the day of Sanford's early season 43-36 cat-and-mouse win on Evans' home court.

And as this season would illustrate numerous times, there was no sure bet on how rematches would turn out. Yet another example of that unpredictability came when Evans entered the Tribe's gym on the night of February 12th. Earlier in the day the latest Florida Prep Class 4-A High School Basketball Poll was released. Seminole High bumped up a notch to the number four position, placing an even bigger target on the backs of the Tribe for the Trojans to shoot for. My Tuesday night game story reflected just how differently the ball could bounce from one game to the next.

What a difference two months make.

The Evans Trojans trekked to the Seminole High gym Tuesday night, looking to avenge an early season loss to Bill Payne's Fighting Seminoles.

But celebrating the rematch, two months to the exact date of their first encounter, it was the state's fourth-ranked Tribe that did the anniversary celebrating.

After playing cat-and-mouse for three quarters, as Evans had forced Seminole to do back on December 12 in the Trojan gym, Glenn Stambaugh and Bruce McCray triggered a five-minute offensive explosion that lifted the Sanford team to a stunningly decisive 64-39 victory. It was the Tribe's 24th win of the season against one loss.

"Before the game, we talked about playing to our full potential," advised game-high scorer Bruce McCray.

"We got a little hot and finally exploded in the last four minutes."

The Seminoles did more than explode. After being pulled out of its run-and-gun rhythm, senior guard Glenn Stambaugh came up with back-to-back steals that he converted into layups, one a three-point play after drawing a foul.

Stambaugh's defensive gems sparked the rest of the Seminoles at 5:05 of the fourth quarter as Payne's troops busted open the game by outscoring Evans 23-8 down the stretch to ice the victory.

123

Even Trojan coach Dick Hullette's timeout efforts to freeze Stambaugh at the charity stripe didn't do much good. His timeout turned into a five-minute circus as the frustrated Evans coach complained to officials about foreign objects being tossed onto the court by fans.

One of the foreign objects that provided many of the Trojan frustrations in the final period was Seminole senior forward David Thomas. The lanky leaper snagged four fourth-quarter rebounds to help the fast-break plans of the Tribe and canned eight of his 13 points to put the game out of reach.

While Stambaugh was stealing and Thomas was rebounding, it was the presence of McCray in the third period that gave Tribe fans indications of things to come. After being hampered by three first-half personals, McCray came on strong in the third stanza to pump in 10 of his game-high 25 points. The Tribe forward also played havoc with Evans on the boards as he snared a game-high 13 rebounds and dished out four assists.

"I think we showed them that we could play, and play our way," said a pleased McCray as he reflected on the December 12th 43-36 slow-down victory by the Tribe.

"We had a little discussion at half time," pointed out Tribe boss Bill Payne.

"They were knocking us around on the boards and you can't go if you don't rebound."

After a stern tongue-lashing at intermission, the Tribe got going, outrebounding Evans by a two-to-one margin in the second half.

"We don't like playing against that four corners offense that everyone plays in the Metro Conference," added Payne. "It slows us

down too much and throws us out of the type of game we like to play."

The inside game of McCray and Thomas was nicely complimented by Reggie Butler's efforts. The Tribe's 6-6 enforcer collected eight rebounds to go along with his eight points.

Stambaugh's running mate, Keith Whitney, provided the quickness to get the fast break going and added six points, four of them coming in the final stages of the game.

"Our defense was the difference between this game and the first time we played them at their place," observed Payne.

"We put a lot more pressure on the ball in the front court. If you can put good pressure on the guards in the four corners offense, you'll force some turnovers and force the pace of the play."

The Evans offensive performance was unusual. Only three players managed to put points on the board. The Trojan efforts were led by sweet-shooting junior guard Kenny Grant who settled for 20 of the Trojan's 39 points by connecting on numerous parking lot jumpers.

Scott Consoli added 12 points for Evans while the only other Trojan to score was Mike Carter who tallied a lone bucket.

The Seminoles outscored Evans in every period, holding the Trojans to just eight points in the second quarter to head for the locker room with a 26-21 halftime lead.

As usual, the third period began making the difference in the ballgame as the Tribe outscored Evans 15-10 before blasting out to their 23-8 difference in the final period.

The win over Evans marked the 24th on the season for Seminole and completed the Tribe's perfect 6-0 record against Metro Conference teams, no small feat in Central Florida basketball circles.

Payne's Seminoles would have just two more games left on the schedule before the much-anticipated rematch against the only team to set them back, the Daytona Beach Mainland Buccaneers. Mainland's record remained unblemished and Seminole High's nemesis was now ranked second in the state. The rematch would fall on the final night of the regular season Five Star Conference schedule, and a week away from the all-important District 9 Tournament, which would dictate which team from District 9 would advance to the first round of Florida State Basketball Championship play.

CHAPTER 14
Senior Night and Accolades

Rolling off the big win over Evans, Seminole would hit the road in search of win number 25 on the season, then return to the friendly confines of the Sanford High gym for its final home contest of the year, celebrating each season with a special focus on the senior members of the squad.

Much earlier in the season Sanford had rudely welcomed the Apopka Blue Darters to their first season playing in the Five Star Conference by spanking them on the Tribe's home-court 97-60. The game marked the second time in the season Bill Payne's senior-laden team had tied the school record for most points in a single game.

Following the 30-minute bus ride up State Highway 436 just over the Orange/Seminole County line, the Tribe would secure its 25th win of the season. But Apopka, as promised by their coach, Butch Helms following the first beat down, would play better.

"We were outclassed in that first game," stated Helms after Seminole's first match-up against his team produced a whopping 37-point victory margin.

"But we'll play better against them the next timeout."

Helms was correct, but Seminole still had too much for Apopka, even on the host's home court.

Sanford ran into early foul trouble and held a slim one-point lead at the half 35-34. The tenacious and fired-up Blue Darters kept it close through three quarters before Seminole, as it had done numerous times during the season, found another gear in the fourth period and ignited in an offensive outburst.

As he had done so often, Bruce McCray sparked a 21-8 fourth-quarter surge with six points to help the Tribe ease out of the Apopka gym with a 67-50 victory. Apopka had indeed made good on their coach's promise to play better. Keith Whitney warmed up in the final period as well, tossing in six points of his own to aid the Seminole's effort. McCray would finish the night with a game-high 32 points, Whitney with 12, as only two of the Tribe's starting five managed to hit for double figures.

Apopka was fired up from the opening jump and gave Seminole High a rare battle on the boards.

Fred Griffin challenged Seminole's tall front line by pulling down a game-high 13 rebounds for the Blue Darters.

"They were fired up," acknowledged Payne after the win.

"They had a guy dunk down on Reggie Butler's nose early on and it really got them going."

With win 25 secured, Payne and the Seminoles would keep an eye on the remainder of weekend play as a batch of regular season games would fall into place to determine critical seeding for the impending District 9 Tournament.

But first, his attention would turn to Sanford's final home game Tuesday night, February 19.

Sanford's gym was packed as nine members of the Fighting Seminoles would don their home jerseys for the final game of their careers on Sanford's home court. Senior members Bruce McCray, Glenn Stambaugh, Keith Whitney, David Thomas, Shun Thomas, Reggie Butler, Casey Jones, Joe Baker, and Fred Alexander received thunderous applause during spotlight introductions, accompanied by parents and family members at center court.

"Senior Night is always special," acknowledged Payne of the pre-game ceremonies.

"There's always a bit of good and bad to it. The good is that your kids will soon be graduating and moving on with their lives, going out to do what they are going to do. The bad is that you have to say goodbye."

And then with a chuckle, he added a little extra from a coaching perspective as well.

"The bad is that the shelf would be a little bare for the next year. I might be a little insane for carrying nine seniors."

With pre-game festivities concluded, the Tribe got down to business. Earlier in the day the latest Class 4-A High School Basketball Poll had been released. Seminole bumped up a notch and was now ranked third in the state, one spot behind nemesis Daytona Beach Mainland at number two.

It was a memorable night for the seniors to protect their ranking and their home turf, depicted in the lead story on Sports Page 1 of *The Sanford Herald* in Wednesday's edition.

One couldn't blame DeLand coach Art Parrisi and his Bulldogs if they felt they spent Tuesday night in a revolving door. Seminole coach Bill Payne turned loose his departing seniors before a packed "Parent's Night" crowd in a constantly changing lineup.

The end result was a convincing 78-57 win before the hometown folks in the Tribe's last home game of the season. The win boosted the state's third-ranked team to a sparkling 26-1 slate heading into the season finale against Daytona Beach Mainland Friday night.

129

The Bulldogs took the spotlight in the first four minutes of the contest before Bruce McCray canned a rebound for the first Tribe bucket. From there it was all downhill for Parissi and company, who earlier this year stated Seminole didn't have the guards to beat Mainland.

Whether it was revenge or just plain old hankerin' to do good in front of the home crowd, Seminole's guards did just fine thank you.

Glenn Stambaugh accounted for 16 points, all but two coming on his sweet jumper, while speedy Keith Whitney left DeLand dazzled as he continually broke the Bulldog press for 10 points and six assists.

As usual, fellow senior Bruce McCray was on the receiving end of those assists, once again pacing the Seminoles with 27 points. With "Senior Power" as the battle cry, center Reggie Butler and forward David Thomas took care of the boards. Their first-quarter performance enabled Payne's troops to take a 20-14 lead after falling behind early.

Thomas pulled down eight boards and dished out five assists of his own in addition to hitting for seven points while Butler canned another six points and snared eight rebounds.

All but one of Seminole's graduating seniors got into the scoreboard. Shun Thomas, Joe Baker, and Casey Jones managed to score for the Tribe.

"It's great the way that everybody got in the game the way they did," a happy Payne commented about his revolving door lineup. "I've said time and time again that we have five very good starters, but we also have a lot of kids on the bench who can come in and do a good job for us."

The Bulldogs never really threatened in the contest after blowing their first-quarter lead. Stambaugh, Thomas, and Whitney saw to that by combining for 17 of the Tribe's 22 points in the second quarter as the home team took a 42-31 lead into the locker room at the half.

"We forced the pace more this time around," Payne pointed out.

"At their place earlier in the season they dictated the flow of the game."

With a "Parent's Night" victory firmly in their back pockets, Sanford High had completed a memorable season on their home court with just one blemish, the three-point loss to Daytona Beach Mainland, and now stood at 26-1 on the season.

And with elevated state rankings, and seedings for the impending District 9 Tournament a week away at stake, their final road trip to the Buccaneers' tiny home gym that Friday night, took on ever larger dimensions. It seemed both impossible and improbable that the state's second and third-ranked prep basketball teams would be facing each other in a regular-season finale.

The importance of the game did not escape the attention of local Sanford radio station WTRR. A familiar bench mate at the scorer's table seated to my left on game nights was radio play-by-play announcer Joe Johnson. The station had broadcast many of the Tribe's home games during the season and had made the decision to pack up equipment, have broadcast phone lines installed in the Daytona Beach Mainland gym, and broadcast the critical rematch between Payne's squad and the Buccaneers of coach Dick Toth.

It was no small consideration on the part of the radio station, as broadcast phone lines represented a significant cost to WTRR. And symbolic of small-town radio stations, Johnson, the Voice of the

Seminoles, wore more than one hat in the Sanford community.

By day, Johnson served as a minister at the Sanford Christian Church on West Airport Boulevard in the city. By night he traded his bible for headphones and a microphone. Friday night, from the Mainland gym that barely accommodated 1,000, he would take to the airwaves and have his largest radio congregation of the season back home in Sanford.

"Support from station management has been great this season," explained a happy Johnson.

"Usually, we don't carry the road games because of the cost of the telephone lines. But the station and the local merchants have stepped up. Everybody knows what a big game this is for the Seminoles."

CHAPTER 15
The Raucous Rematch

The regular season rematch between Florida's second and third-ranked high school basketball teams required no hype. When Seminole High traveled to the minuscule gym of the Daytona Beach Mainland Buccaneers on the night of February 22nd, virtually every central Florida prep basketball fan was expecting to see two high school heavyweights go at it from the opening jump ball in a game with the weight of a Muhammad Ali-Joe Frazier rematch of the mid-1970s hanging in the air.

And with good reason. The host Buccaneers and the visiting Fighting Seminoles arrived on the final Friday night of the regular season with identical 26-1 records. Their initial encounter was a memorable 15-round slugfest earlier in the year when Mainland emerged with a three-point win on the judges' scorecards at 78-75.

On paper, this would be the high school basketball equivalent of *Rocky II*, released in theaters during the Summer of 1979. It would be Rocky Balboa versus Apollo Creed in high tops played on the hardwood. If you could get your hands on one of just 1,000 game tickets available, it would be an entertainment bargain at just $2.00 for the price of admission.

Outside of seeking revenge for their earlier season loss to Mainland even more was at stake this time around. The final game of the regular season would determine seedings for the District-9 Tournament that would get underway the following Wednesday night, February 28th. A Mainland win would secure the top seed for the Buccaneers. A Seminole victory would mean a tie for the Conference Championship between the two teams. If Seminole

High evened the score against Mainland, it would be the old-school methodology to determine which team was seeded number one and which was seeded number two. The names of the two schools would be placed in a hat with an old fashion draw to settle things.

"There's really nothing different about this one than the first game," confided Seminole coach Bill Payne during that Friday morning's phone interview.

Once again, the key to the outcome would be the performance of two of Central Florida's premier prep players, Sanford's forward Bruce McCray and Mainland's guard Sam Henry.

"We certainly don't want to let Sam Henry score 32 points again," offered Payne in his pre-game assessment.

"He's good. We're going to have to control him better than we did the first time around."

Payne's coaching counterpart at Lake Howell offered a fresh scouting report on the Buccaneers' talented guard.

"We played them last week and lost by 14 points at their place," offered Silver Hawk skipper Greg Robinson.

"I really think that if Seminole can keep Sam Henry away from the ball a little more, and if Sanford's starting five can play as well against Mainland as they've played against us, they can win, even if the game is on the road."

Another key would be the continued emergence of the Tribe's leading scorer Bruce McCray, who had slowly transformed into a different type of player since the first ballgame against Mainland.

In the final two weeks of the season, McCray had turned in perhaps the best all-around performances of any player in the Five

Star Conference. Over that stretch, he averaged 24 points per game, improved his defense, and was hitting the boards more aggressively, lending aid to the Tribe's other front-line starters, forward David Thomas and center Reggie Butler.

Butler had been going to the hoop with more success and confidence coming down the season's home stretch. Added offense from him would take some of the pressure off McCray to score and would also cause potential problems for Mainland in the backcourt.

In the first meeting, Seminole guards Glenn Stambaugh and Keith Whitney had little problem in solving the Buccaneers' vaunted press. The problem was costly turnovers once they got the ball to the frontcourt.

A better performance from McCray and more offensive involvement from Butler could play a role in a different outcome from game one. Guard play would likewise be a critical factor. It was Whitney's surprisingly accurate jumpers and Stambaugh's nothing-but-net bombs from the wing that brought Seminole back into the first game after trailing by 14 points in the third period.

"That first Mainland game was the first time I came down the court and just shot automatically," shared Stambaugh.

"And it felt good."

One area Payne didn't think he needed to be concerned about was facing the distractions of Mainland's home crowd.

"We had fans hanging from the rafters in our place the first game, and there was plenty of noise," he pointed out.

"Their gym holds about half-as-many people as ours. We have to play at their place for the District Tournament, so we're not going to let the crowd bother us."

So, the table was set for the Friday night tipoff at 8 p.m. The only question that remained: would the rematch, could the rematch, live up to the heart-stopping 78-75 finish of Round One between the Buccaneers and the Seminoles?

My Saturday morning headline and story in *The Sanford Herald* illustrated that it painfully did not for Seminole High.

"Mainland Mauls Tribe in Rematch 80-60"

It was billed as the rematch of the season. But Friday night's long-awaited showdown between second-ranked Daytona Mainland and third-ranked Sanford needed a new title after 32 minutes of basketball.

"The Mr. Sam Henry Show" would have been a little more appropriate.

The Buccaneers all-state senior guard candidate shot, passed, dribbled, and hustled circles around the Seminoles Friday night before a packed home crowd in the cracker-box Buccaneers gym. Mainland's crew gave Sanford a sound basketball lesson.

When class was dismissed, much to the dismay of a loyal Sanford following, the Buccaneers had graduated with a convincing 80-60 victory.

"This is home to us," beamed an ecstatic Buc coach Dick Toth.

"We haven't lost here all year. The kids don't like anybody coming in here and having their way."

As they did in the first match-up, in which Mainland squeezed out a three-point 78-75 win on the Seminole's home court, they let the

Tribe have its way early for the grand total of four minutes.

Senior forward Bruce McCray found the range early for six quick points off a pair of nifty assists from Keith Whitney and another from David Thomas.

Then, Henry, Larry Prince, and Herb Davis responded as if on cue.

The slick shooting Henry canned three long jumpers and began dishing out some of his game-high 14 assists on the night to help Mainland knot the score at 12-all a minute and a half later. His passing performance claimed the career assist record for the Bucs at 304. His roundball wizardry helped Mainland smash the single season winning record as they finished the regular season at 27-1.

Their only loss came on a neutral court during a three-game week in which the Bucs faced Daytona nemesis Seabreeze High, Sanford, and 1A powerhouse Daytona Beach Warner Christian all within a five- day-span.

With Henry passing and shooting, the Bucs moved out to a 33-27 halftime lead and the frenzied home crowd called for blood.

Henry, Prince, and Harris delivered by pushing the Buccaneers to a 10-point lead early in the third period and never let up as the Seminoles continually squandered opportunities to pull themselves back into the game.

Twice Sanford came down the court and put up four shots. And twice they missed all four.

"We couldn't get it in the hoop and Henry didn't miss," said a disturbed Payne, whose squad stood a chance of meeting the Buccaneers yet a third time in the following week's District 9 Tournament.

Mainland canned 35 of 61 shots on the evening for a blistering 57 percent while the Seminoles managed to connect on just 22 of 56 for 40 percent, their worst shooting effort of the season.

"We beat them at their place, and we beat them at home. I think that should prove something," a happy Toth stated after the game.

Payne agreed with his rival's assessment.

"Everybody is saying the third time is a charm. Well, how about the sixth time?" Payne asked.

"That same group beat us twice as JV's, twice last year and twice this year. They are simply an outstanding basketball team. I don't know if we're capable of beating them."

The lone Seminole who turned in a respectable performance was Bruce McCray, whom the Bucs handled well in the first game. After early foul trouble, McCray came on to score 25 points, but it was not enough to offset Henry's game-high 27 combined with 19 points from Prince and 15 from Jerry Smith.

Seminole's backcourt partners Glenn Stambaugh and Keith Whitney came up with 10 and 13 points respectively, but it was much too little too late.

The Bucs will now take on Lake Brantley in Wednesday's opening round of the district tournament, an event that Toth and his Buccaneers have already laid out a game plan.

"If the tournament runs true to form, we'll probably meet Sanford again," pointed out Mainland's coach.

"It's tough to beat a team like Seminole three times. They are a good ball club, certainly better than the 20-point difference tonight. But we came of age this evening."

While Toth's Buccaneers were coming of age and securing the top seed for the District-9 Tournament, the Seminoles were left with a long, silent 40-mile bus ride in the dark back to Sanford. And they were also left wondering how, if at all, they could solve Daytona Beach Mainland. The 20-point loss did more than wound their pride and damage their psyche. It added another obstacle to making it to the first round of state playoffs. Now a second seed and scheduled to face Apopka on the second night of opening round action the following Thursday, Bill Payne's Fighting Seminoles would be forced to regroup, rebound, and pick themselves up off the canvas. And they would now have to win three games over three nights and find some kind of magical formula in the next week for a potential third clash with Daytona Beach Mainland. They would be grasping for a "Seventh Time Is a Charm" miracle to break Mainland's six-game winning streak against them.

And news that reached the Tribe Tuesday of tournament week did little to bolster their confidence or mend their wounded pride.

CHAPTER 16
Setting The Tournament Table

In the four-day run-up to opening night of the District 9 Basketball Tournament, there would be plenty to write about both on and off the court.

And while final tournament seedings would not be determined until Tuesday of that week, my February 26th afternoon column in *The Sanford Herald* would run down a checklist of items taking place.

First among them is the latest Florida Class 4-A Basketball Poll release. On the heels of their 20-point shellacking at the hands of nemesis Daytona Beach Mainland the previous Friday night, the once third-ranked Sanford Seminoles woke up Monday morning to find they had disappeared. Poof. Gone from sight and nowhere to be found ranked among the state's top 10 prep teams.

Now granted, it seemed perfectly reasonable for the Tribe to fall in the poll based on that loss, maybe even to the bottom of the top 10. But still, they had a 26-2 record and lost to a team ranked above them. It seemed unconscionable that they would slip so far in the poll to not even be listed in the "also receiving votes" category.

I placed a few phone calls to my sports writing buddies around the state to find out the rationale for dropping Seminole High totally out of the rankings. Without naming names or pointing fingers, the prevailing opinion of many who voted in the poll came to this collective conclusion.

"Sanford Seminole can't beat Mainland. Why keep them ranked when they won't even make it out of their District?"

I called Bill Payne that Tuesday morning to get his reaction.

"I really don't know what to say about the poll," he responded in our phone interview.

"I don't pay that much attention to polls. We're trying to get ready for Thursday night. I know the kids talk about the polls, the fans talk about the polls, that's just part of the game."

But I could hear the consternation and irritation in his voice as he had a handful of days to put a band-aid on his team's damaged frame of mind and prepare for his first-round tournament opponent.

Although the tournament site, the tiny Mainland High gym, had been decided before the season even began, howls of concern now arose over the size of the facility and its limited seating capacity. There would be eight teams competing over the four nights, and once space was set aside to accommodate staff, the press, and visiting teams, there would be only about 900 tickets available for each game night. Many students, fans, and community followers would have little to no chance of seeing their respective teams in tournament play.

Those issues were compounded even more once Wednesday night's opening-round games began. During the week of the tournament, it turned unusually cold by Florida standards. Temperatures that Wednesday and Thursday night dipped into the high 20s. That might be considered a heat wave in Buffalo for that time of year, but Floridians trade in their flip-flops and t-shirts for fur coats and parkas once the temperature slips below 60.

The limited physical space leading into the gym added more calamity to creature comforts. The concession area of the Buccaneers' facility was adjacent to the ticket booth. There was hardly enough room to turn around without knocking into your elbows. If a fan wanted a hot dog or hot chocolate at intermission, they had to stand outside in the cold to drink or eat their snacks. And it doesn't take long for 29 degrees to take the "hot" out of both hotdogs and hot chocolate.

As the tournament unfolded, the logistics of just getting in and out of the gym would become a nightmare. Even the teams themselves, especially those playing the nightcap games, were forced to wait outside until 20 minutes before game time to get in. The situation prompted one of Lyman's athletic trainers to quip, "I'll just tape up my guy's ankles one by one out here in the arctic tundra parking lot."

Those issues aside, by Tuesday morning of tournament week, the seedings had been finalized, although there really were no surprises, chief among them that host Daytona Beach Mainland drew the number one seed and would face Lake Brantley, and Lyman would meet Spruce Creek the first night of the tournament.

Seminole High, which drew the second seed, and in the bracket opposite of Mainland, would tangle with improved Apopka in the 7 p.m. Thursday contest while Lake Howell would finish off opening round games by matching up against DeLand at 8:30.

District tournaments are, in reality, basketball's version of a "do-over." Despite won-loss records and seedings, they give every team a fresh slate and a final opportunity to become a roundball David slaying a basketball Goliath. Over time, that was the precise reason the NCAA Basketball Tournament had justifiably earned the nickname "March Madness," popularized by CBS hoops announcer Brent Musburger during the 1982 college tourney. For the record, "March Madness" was historically first used by Illinois basketball official Henry V. Porter in 1939 to describe high school tournaments in Illinois.

Musburger updated the term on live television to perfectly describe North Carolina's thrilling 63-62 win over Georgetown in a chess match between two of the greatest coaches in the college ranks at that time, Dean Smith and John Thompson. It was the perfect ending to a slate of 47 games played that year in the Louisiana Superdome.

So as the Five Star Conference/District 9 coaches were prepping their teams for Central Florida's version of "March Madness," I placed my phone calls for that week's tournament preview story in *The Sanford Herald.* And the story carried a headline reflective of that "clean slate" and "do-overs."

It's The Start of a Brand-New Season

Toss out the regular season records and pay no heed to past performances. It's tournament time for District 9, and as most coaches like to refer to it, "It's a brand-new season."

Mainland High School's cracker-box gymnasium, with a whopping 1,000 seating capacity, will be the site for the four-day tournament that opens with first-round action Wednesday night and runs through Saturday's championship game.

At stake is a chance for the winner to advance to the first round of state playoffs in regional competition.

Four major questions will be answered by Saturday night. Can top-seeded Mainland continue to waltz through the rest of the Five Star Conference? Can the Sanford Seminoles rebound from a 20-point loss to Mainland and challenge the Bucs for a state playoff berth? Will a regular season also-ran rise from the pack and pull off an upset? And finally, can anybody find a ticket and a seat for the games?

Final tournament seedings weren't set until Monday afternoon. Wednesday's games will pit the Lyman Greyhounds at 6-8 against the Spruce Creek hawks at 7-7, while top-seed and second-in-the-state-ranked Mainland meets eighth-seeded Lake Brantley at 4-10.

Both the Lyman Greyhounds and Spruce Creek Hawks have experienced ups and downs this season. That contest is perhaps the most up in the air as far as a favorite is concerned.

"I feel confident about Spruce Creek," commented Lyman greyhound coach Tom Lawrence.

"They've been up and down like us so we will have to play well. We're in the same bracket as Mainland so we will really have to put it together in the tournament."

Mainland, meanwhile, is a heavy favorite over the Patriots. Something that Lake Brantley coach Bob Peterson is well aware of.

"We will have to get a lot of breaks," admits Peterson of the Wednesday encounter about his team's chances for an upset.

"But we aren't going to roll over and play dead, either. I'm telling our kids to go out and enjoy the game and play their best. Mainland is a fine basketball team, but by the same token, we have everything to gain and nothing to lose."

Peterson used the recent weekend example of what role emotion can play in sports.

"Look at what the college kids did in the Olympics when they won the gold medal. That's got to say something about emotionalism

and team play. That was great to see."

(Peterson was referring to the incredible "Miracle on Ice," that had taken place in Lake Placid just a few days earlier, when ABC's Al Michaels exuberantly asked a worldwide audience, "Do You Believe in Miracles?" It was a rhetorical question that put into perspective the U.S. men's hockey team's 4-3 victory over the heavily favored four-time defending gold medal champion Russians. Led by coach Herb Brooks, Mike Eruzione, and goalie Jim Craig, *Sports Illustrated* magazine would later label the February 22, 1980, game the best international hockey story in the past 100 years).

In Thursday's lid-lifter at 7 p.m., Bill Payne's Fighting Seminoles at 12-2, take on one of the conference's most improved teams in the last half of the season, Apopka.

"I'd say the Blue Darters and Lake Howell could be labeled the tournament sleepers," commented Payne.

"Right now, we don't really care whom we play."

When queried as to how his team would bounce back from an 80-60 loss to Mainland in the final regular season game, Payne replied bluntly, "Our kids are going to bounce back, we will prove no team is 20 points better than us."

Thursday's night-capper at 8:30 features the other tournament dark horse, Lake Howell at 7-7 in a match-up against 4-10 Deland.

Next to the top two seeds, the Silver Hawks are the hottest team coming into the tournament, having clinched six victories in the last eight games.

Despite its hot finish and favorite's role, Lake Howell coach Greg Robinson cautioned his squad against looking ahead.

"We finished well because we finally found some intensity," commented the Hawks hoop boss.

"But DeLand hasn't really put it together this season, either.

"We can't look ahead to the second game, or we won't get past the first."

So, the preview story was done and put to bed. Time for the talking to be over and the playing to start. Or so I thought.

Not five minutes after press manager Frank Voltoline hit the green power button at precisely 4:40 and *The Sanford Herald's* presses came to life that afternoon, I happened to have a second conversation with Payne, and it tied into Greg Robinson's comments about looking ahead.

The fact of the matter was, outside of the customary pre-tournament comments to reporters, both Payne and Mainland High's coach Dick Toth had a strong inkling they would indeed tangle a third time that season in the forthcoming Saturday night District Championship game.

Toth had earlier hinted as much by commenting following his Buccaneers' big 80-60 win over Sanford, "If the tournament runs true to form, we will probably see Seminole High a third time this season. A team like Seminole is hard to beat three times in one season."

In our second conversation that day, Payne too confessed a third meeting with Mainland was on his and his team's minds.

"We weren't trying to look past our opening game against Apopka, but it was hard not to look ahead," he admitted.

"I was looking ahead, and the kids were looking ahead. Every player on this team is a competitor. They don't back down, and they challenge each other every day in practice even in routine stuff like wind sprints and suicide drills. They wanted another shot at Mainland and quite frankly, before the tournament started, they were more confident than I was that we would get it."

And he confided that he had been searching for a tool or strategy that could possibly change the outcome if the Buccaneers and Seminoles indeed met a third time for the District Championship.

He had reached deep into his coaching bag of tricks and over the four days leading up to the tournament, had been phasing in aspects of basketball's "triangle-and-two" defense. It was an unusual defensive scheme he had only used perhaps six times in his previous coaching seasons.

Sanford had traditionally mixed a two-one-two zone or a pressing man-to-man defense throughout the course of a very successful season. But Mainland posed a different challenge that called for a different solution.

Off the record, Payne explained the "triangle-and-two" might work against Mainland if his Seminoles could execute it well and consistently.

Harkening back to his earlier comments about Mainland's outside shooting ability, Payne had to find a way to limit the damage done by Mainland's perimeter proficiency. In the recent 20-point loss to the Buccaneers, Mainland had played bombs away from the outside, scorching the nets by shooting 57 percent from the floor.

"Man, we knew Sam Henry could shoot, but their whole team, even their big guys had great outside skill," he elaborated.

147

And he further explained the "triangle-and-two" was designed to accomplish three things: First, it put more direct outside pressure on the ball with three players forming a perimeter triangle that would float back and forth following ball movement and keep a hand in the face of at least two of Mainland's three deadly outside shooters. That would be the responsibility of guards Glenn Stambaugh and Keith Whitney. In an unusual twist, center Reggie Butler would abandon the paint and play near the top of the key to complete the "triangle" and to shadow Mainland center Herb Harris, who had an incredibly soft touch for a big man from 25 feet out and was averaging 16 points on the season. Second, if the strategy worked and Mainland adjusted its outside game to come inside, it would be the responsibility of forwards Bruce McCray and David Thomas to step into any holes created in the floating zone to challenge shots from the 12-to-15-foot range. Third, it would challenge high passes from the Mainland guards to their big men playing down low under the boards.

During the season, Seminole had not used the defense at all, and while the strategy seemed plausible on paper and in theory, there was no guarantee it would work for the Tribe against Mainland in a Saturday night championship title.

But first, it was "March Madness" time. And both Daytona Beach Mainland and the Sanford Seminoles had to avoid any tournament land mines to get to Saturday night.

CHAPTER 17
Not Seminole County's Opening Night

At least on the opening night of the District 9 Tournament, as predicted by Buccaneers coach Dick Toth, the event ran true to form. The details were profiled in my first-round game story in *The Sanford Herald* which illustrated a game that could have gone either way between Lyman and Spruce Creek went Spruce Creek's way, and unfortunately for Lake Brantley coach Bob Peterson and his Patriots, there would be no basketball version of a "Miracle on Ice."

After opening round action Wednesday night of the District-9 Class 4A men's basketball tournament, Volusia County prep squads hold a two-zip edge over their Seminole County rivals.

The Spruce Creek Hawks and top-seeded Mainland Buccaneers earned semi-final berths Wednesday night and a shot at taking another step toward the state playoffs.

Spruce Creek came up with 11 unanswered points in a three-minute stretch late in the final period to edge Lyman's Greyhounds 54-50. Mainland's victory came a little easier, 84-56 at the expense of outmanned Lake Brantley.

Lyman jumped out to a slim lead in the first quarter over Spruce Creek behind a hot-handed Neal Gillis. The slick-shooting junior forward canned a pair of floor shots and was perfect from the charity stripe to help Tom Lawrence's squad forge a 14-11 advantage.

The tables turned on Lyman in the second period, however, as the Greyhounds were whistled for eight team fouls in three minutes and Lyman was forced to go to its bench early.

Guard Shawn Britton and 6-8 center Thomas Tenbroeck canned six points each in the second period to help Spruce Creek knot the score at 38-all by the intermission.

The Hawks pushed ahead by four points heading into the final period and then rattled off the first 11 points in stanza number four to put the game out of reach despite a desperate charge by the Greyhounds.

Britton paced Spruce Creek with 14 points while Neal Gillis led Lyman's efforts with 22 markers.

In the nightcap game of the opening round, Lake Brantley blitzed out in front of Mainland's top-seeded Buccaneers 8-2 only to have the roof cave in.

Sparked by all-state candidate guard Sam Henry and center Herb Harris, the Bucs outscored Lake Brantley 37-4 over the next seven minutes to put the game out of reach by halftime.

In holding the Patriots to four second-quarter points, Mainland built a 39-12 lead at the half and finished the night freely substituting.

The Bucs stretched the margin to 60-29 by the end of the third period and finished the night with an 84-56 win over the game but outsized Lake Brantley crew.

Senior guard Doug Dershimer led the Patriot effort with 21 points while Mainland placed four players in double figures. Henry scored 20, Harris netted 15, Larry Prince added 13, while Jerry Smith scored 10 points, all coming on ally-oop passes from Henry to pace the Mainland offense.

"We took advantage of early opportunities but then we lost concentration," commented Lake Brantley coach Bob Peterson.

"We had the shots but couldn't get them in. Then their big men started hitting shots and started hitting the boards. It's difficult to prepare for Mainland's size when you're as small as we are and don't have any size to practice against."

Mainland coach Dick Toth seemed almost as happy about the tournament pairings as he was with the one-sided victory.

"We now have the night off before we have to play again," observed Toth."

"If the tournament runs as it should and we have to play Seminole again, they'll have to play three straight nights to win this tournament.

But Toth wasn't looking too far ahead.

"We've got Spruce Creek next, and they get up for us and play us tough. Anytime you go against a coach like Spruce Creek's Joe Pigotte, you have to be prepared for anything.

"He's been coaching for something like 20 years and knows how to prepare for a game."

The Mainland coach was also pleased about the opportunity to go to his bench.

"We're trying to find a strong eighth man," he pointed out.

"If we win the tournament and get into regional and state competition, we have to have that kind of depth to keep going."

The Buc boss complimented his reserves on their fourth quarter role.

"Sometimes there isn't enough credit given to our players because people are so used to the good plays, they make the fans seem to lose sight of how exceptional the kids really are.

"Our fans have come to expect near-perfect play every time we go out on the court."

So, opening night had come and gone with no real surprises. And the table was set for the second round of games Thursday and an indication if Sanford's team had the wherewithal to shake off the drubbing they took from Mainland a short five days ago.

CHAPTER 18

Gaudreau's Generous Gesture

For 28 games that basketball season, senior guard Glenn Stambaugh's familiar jersey #24 could be seen gliding up and down the floor, launching 25-foot jump shots, playing solid defense, helping fellow guard Keith Whitney break defensive presses and was pure money from the foul line.

Since arriving from Lyman that summer, he had worked and earned his place of trust on the Seminole's roster. Better still, he had become gold from the outside and could hit clutch shots seemingly without breaking a sweat. If Seminole coach Bill Payne needed an inside basket, Bruce McCray was his man. If Payne needed an outside bomb, Stambaugh had become his go-to guy.

But on the night of Seminole High's opening round game against the Apopka Blue Darters in the District 9 tournament, there was big trouble in the Tribe's teepee.

Payne and the Seminoles had arrived early for their 7 p.m. tipoff, and fans were just beginning to filter into the gym when the coach faced a problem he'd never encountered in his entire career.

He and assistant Tom Smith and team trainer Jim "Doc" Terwilliger, along with statistician Dean Smith were seated next to the scorer's table about to put Seminole High's player lineup into the official tournament scorebook when Stambaugh came out of the visiting team's locker where the Seminoles were suiting up before pre-game warm-ups.

Stambaugh was in street clothes, his shoulders slumped and his head down. When Payne looked up to his approaching guard, he could tell something was off.

"Coach," Stambaugh almost whispered. "I've got a problem."

"What's the matter, Glenn," Payne inquired.

"I brought the wrong uniform," choked out his ace shooter.

Stambaugh had indeed made the mistake of packing his white jersey #24 and matching shorts. The only problem was, Seminole was the designated road team that night, and his fellow team-mates had correctly packed their black road uniforms for the game.

Payne was speechless for a moment, probably unsure whether he wanted to hug Stambaugh in consolation or place his hands around the young guard's throat to choke him. Then he said the only thing he could say.

"Glenn, the rules are you have to have the correct uniform to be in the game. I'm sorry, but you can't be on the floor with the wrong uniform. You can't play tonight, you'll have to sit this one out."

"I know, responded Stambaugh softly. I'm sorry."

Payne was left to just shake his head as his smooth-shooting senior quietly wheeled and slowly walked back to the Seminole's locker room.

He and his staff were left to figure out how to compensate for having their best outside shot absent from the starting lineup in now, the most important game of the year. The discussion became animated when just a few minutes before official warm-up time began for both teams, another figure approached the trio. This time it was reserve guard Mike Gaudreau.

Gaudreau too was in street clothes, and by this time he should have been in his warm-up sweats getting ready for pre-game layups and shooting practice. Gaudreau wore jersey #20 that season but as a junior his playing time was limited by the two senior guards in front of him, Stambaugh and Whitney. But Gaudreau could play, and like Stambaugh, possessed a very good outside shooting touch.

Gaudreau eyed Payne and said, "Coach, I want to give Glenn my jersey. He's got to play tonight. He's got to be in the lineup."

Payne gently shook his head and responded, "Mike, no. I can't ask you or tell you to sacrifice your uniform so another player can play. That's just not something I can do or want to do."

But Gaudreau persisted. He was the kind of kid every coach would want on his team, and he bled Seminole High orange and black.

"Coach, I'm giving Glenn my uniform. He's got to be on the court tonight."

"Mike, that's a decision only you can make, and I'm not asking or telling you to make it," Payne responded again.

Gaudreau nodded his head in acknowledgment of his coach's message, wheeled, and returned to the locker room like Stambaugh.

Minutes later, when the team emerged for pre-game warm-ups, Stambaugh was wearing Gaudreau's jersey # 20, while Gaudreau pulled up a seat on the Seminole bench, sitting in his warm-up sweats but with no uniform underneath.

Payne incredulously shook his head at Gaudreau's selfless act and quietly walked over to the scorer's table to adjust Stambaugh's jersey number from his customary #24 to Gaudreau's sacrificed #20.

At that moment, no Hollywood scriptwriter could have ever imagined or conjured up a storyline to suggest just how monumental Gaudreau's gesture even remotely would become that night.

155

But 32 minutes of high school basketball later, by giving up his jersey so Stambaugh could play, Gaudreau literally and figuratively saved the Fighting Seminoles' season.

"March Madness" had indeed struck that night. During my 40-minute ride back to *The Sanford Herald* to file my game story following the conclusion of the nightcap game, I was talking to myself.

"How in God's name do I tell the story of what happened tonight?" I kept thinking over and over.

"How do I even write the lead paragraph?"

For some unknown reason, a baseball poem by Earnest L. Thayer kept popping into my mind. I hated poetry and suffered through two solid weeks of it in high school sophomore English class. I hated poetry until Ms. Florence Blankenship, my English teacher who would recruit me to become sports editor of my high school newspaper, *The Roundtable* at Kellam High in Virginia Beach, introduced me to a baseball poem entitled, "Casey at the Bat."

The poem described the desperate efforts of the fictitious "Mudville" baseball team to win a game with their legendary hero "Casey" coming to the plate trailing in the game and stepping into the batter's box down to the team's final out.

I became so enamored with the poem that I committed it to memory and now, nine years after being subjected to sophomore-year high school poetry, the poem's opening stanza kept playing through my head as I navigated I-95 and I-4 home to Sanford.

"The outlook wasn't brilliant for the Mudville nine that day.

The score stood four to two with, but one inning left to play.

156

And when Cooney died at first, and Barrows did the same,

A sickly silence fell upon the patrons of the game.

A struggling few got up to go in deep despair.

The rest clung to that hope that springs eternal in the human breast.

They thought if only Casey could get a whack at that—

We'd put up even money now with Casey at the bat."

Somehow, someway, I thought to myself, I've got to paraphrase this poem and turn a baseball situation into a basketball outcome. By the time I reached *The Sanford Herald* and sat down before my Underwood manual to hack out my story, I had my lead, with paraphrasing pardons and citations credited to Earnest L. Thayer.

It looked extremely rocky for the Sanford five last night. Apopka held the lead by one and time was oh, so slight. The Darters put the full press on to try to ice the win. Their hopes, their dreams, and their upset plans brought quiet to the gym. But it was Stambaugh, mighty Stambaugh at the free throw line again.

Now there is no joy in Darterville, Apopka has struck out.

Sanford's senior guard Glenn Stambaugh was the right man, at the right time in the right situation Thursday night.

The Tribe's ace charity shooter calmly stepped to the line with, but three seconds left in the game and his team down by one, 46-45.

The 90-percent shooter from the foul line sank both ends of a one-and-one situation to lift Bill Payne's Fighting Seminoles to an exasperating 47-46 victory over Apopka, sending the Tribe into to-

night's semi-final showdown of the District 9 basketball tournament against the Lake Howell Silver Hawks.

Not bad for a guy who almost couldn't suit up because he brought the wrong uniform to the game.

After falling behind early, Apopka battled back against Seminole late in the fourth quarter and took a 46-45 lead with nine seconds to play when center Reggie Butler was whistled for a goal-tending infraction.

The Tribe coach wanted Stambaugh all the way, in hopes of his ace shooter either getting off one of his patented jumpers or drawing a foul. The plan worked to perfection. Guards Stambaugh and Keith Whitney worked the crisscross play under the Apopka basket with David Thomas handling the inbounds pass. Stambaugh got the leather and weaved his way through the Apopka full-court press as precious seconds ticked off the clock.

As Stambaugh came to the top of the key and began to get set for a jumper, a Blue Darter defender slapped the ball away. Unfortunately for coach Butch Helms and his upset-minded squad, the player also slapped Stambaugh.

Helms didn't see the foul.

"It's a shame it had to come down to a loose ball on the floor," commented the Apopka coach.

"I thought we took it to Sanford in the second half. We should have won."

Helms was correct. The Seminoles shot horrendously from the foul line, hitting just 15-30 shots in the game, including a paltry 7-19 in the critical fourth period.

But Stambaugh was the ace up Payne's sleeve. The senior guard had connected on 5 of 5 earlier free throws and finished the night a perfect 7 of 7 from the charity stripe.

Butler, upset at the goal-tending call, had nothing to be upset about at his performance, one of his finest of the season. The slender, soft-spoken big man canned 10 points, but more importantly, ripped 12 rebounds and blocked an amazing eight Blue Darter shots.

Despite being held to seven points on the night, Bruce McCray managed to break the Seminole single-season record for scoring with a total of 613 points; a record of 606 previously set by John Zeuli back in 1974.

If the Seminoles had an unsung hero in the contest, it had to be backup guard Mike Gaudreau who volunteered his #20 jersey so Stambaugh could suit up.

Greg Robinson's Lake Howell Silver Hawks earned a 7 p.m. semi-final berth against Seminole via a 70-58 victory over the Deland Bulldogs.

Mark Layton turned in a surprising 20-point effort to go along with Rusty Conway's 14 and 10 each from guards Larry Mincey and Bruce Brightman to pace the Lake Howell victory.

In the other semi-final game, Daytona Mainland faces Spruce Creek at 8:30 p.m.

"Layton did a super job coming off the bench for us," complimented Robinson.

"Conway played well before fouling out and Brightman gave us a lift late in the game, too."

What does Robinson feel his Silver Hawks have to do to beat Seminole after losing twice to the Tribe in regular season play?

"We have to play the boards with them," pointed out Robinson.

"We out-rebounded Deland 46-32. We need that kind of margin against Seminole. We can't afford to let them play volleyball on the boards."

Sanford radio station WTRR will broadcast the Seminole-Lake Howell game. The pre-game show goes on the air at 6:50 p.m. with play-by-play announcer Joe Johnson.

CHAPTER 19
Running True-To-Form

Daytona Beach Mainland coach Dick Toth turned out to be a pretty good prophet. Outside of the scare that Apopka threw into Seminole High in the opening round, the seedings for the tournament held, and at the conclusion of semi-final action Friday night, the road map for a third confrontation between the Mainland Buccaneers and Sanford Fighting Seminoles had been plotted. My game stories in *The Sanford Herald* from the March 1 semi-finals reflected a true-to-form outcome for the remaining four teams.

To no one's great surprise, the District 9 basketball championship has come down to a rematch between the Daytona Mainland Buccaneers and the Sanford Seminoles.

Bill Payne's squad earned a berth Friday night with a 71-60 win over the Lake Howell Silver Hawks while the top-seeded Mainland Bucs knocked off Spruce Creek 60-48.

Saturday's title clash, which carries with it the right to advance to the regional round of state playoff action, marks the third time the Seminoles and Bucs will collide.

Mainland owns a pair of wins over Sanford, the first coming in a tight three-point 78-75 win, the second in an 80-60 rout.

Seminole appeared much smoother in Friday night's battle against Lake Howell on the heels of their opening round squeaker against Apopka.

The Tribe opened an eight-point lead in the first quarter on the hot outside shooting of guard Keith Whitney and the inside game of Bruce McCray. Behind McCray's eight points in the second stanza and the rebounding of center Reggie Butler, Seminole pushed the margin to 19 at intermission, 42-23.

But Lake Howell had no plans to roll over and play dead.

Behind the torrid shooting of senior forward Reggie Barnes, the Silver Hawks owned the first six minutes of the third period, slicing the Seminole lead to eight points.

The Seminoles regained their composure in the final two minutes of the third and allowed Lake Howell no closer than seven points before eventually wrapping up the semi-final win by 11.

The Tribe placed three players in double figures. Bruce McCray rebounded from a poor performance against Apopka to can a game-high 23 points. Seminole also got something from its backcourt that's been missing the last six games—balanced scoring.

Glenn Stambaugh fired in 20 points, including a 10-11 performance from the free throw line to go along with a 15-point effort from Keith Whitney.

Before fouling out in the final two minutes, Reggie Butler scored just four points but collected 10 rebounds to go along with David Thomas' seven points and eight rebounds.

"Our play on the boards and that stretch where they went way out in front is what killed us," commented Hawk coach Greg Robinson.

"But give Sanford the credit. We played them four times this year and they beat us all four."

Payne too credited his squad with a return to form following a near-disastrous outing against Apopka.

*"The kids played about three good quarters tonight instead of one,"
observed the Seminole boss.*

*"We kept our heads better tonight and just had the stretch at the
start of the second half."*

*Silver Hawk Reggie Barnes was partly to blame. The talented sen-
ior, playing his last game in a Hawk uniform, paced Lake Howell
with 22 points. Bruce Brightman and Rusty Conway also hit double figures with 10 each.*

*After a sticky first quarter, the Mainland Buccaneers had little trou-
ble in handling Spruce Creek's Hawks 60-48.*

*Center Herb Harris scored 17 points to lead a balanced attack that
included 15 from All-State guard candidate Sam Henry and 10
from forward Alvin Payne.*

*Mack Horne sparked the Spruce Creek efforts with 14 points while
Shawn Britton notched 12.*

*"I really don't know what to say about playing Seminole a third
time," commented Mainland coach Dick Toth.*

*"It's tough to beat a team that good three times, especially when
you have to play them twice in just a few days."*

*"We just have to play with intensity every second of the game against
Mainland," countered Payne.*

*"We showed sparks of that intensity tonight against Lake Howell,
especially early in the game."*

*For the winner, a victory means a regional match on Tuesday. For
the loser, the season suddenly comes to an end.*

Mainland enters the contest at 29-1 while the Seminoles carry a

28-2 record into the showdown. Friday night's semi-final win garnered Seminole High a place in the Seminole County sports record books. The Tribe broke the county's single season winning mark with their 28th win, a record previously held by Rick Steinke's 27-2 Lyman Greyhounds during the 1977-78 season.

"I'm in a damned if I do and damned if I don't situation," closed Toth.

"If we win, the team gets the credit because they've been together so long, and this is my first year as coach. If we lose, it's because of me."

Sanford radio station WTRR will once again broadcast the contest. Play-by-play announcer Joe Johnson signs on the air at 7:45 p.m. for the action.

So, the tournament that set up a projected rematch between Mainland and Sanford had, in fact, run true to form. As Payne sat waiting for his team to finish showering up and board the bus for the late-night ride back to Sanford, we chatted for a few minutes about how physically demanding it was to play back-to-back-back games over a three-night stretch. He agreed it was tough and gave a shout-out to team trainer Jim "Doc Terwilleger."

"If there's ever been a guy for all seasons and a jack of all trades," it has to be "Doc," pointed out Payne.

"He's got to be the greatest guy in the world and can be found just about anywhere, at any time, and in any capacity helping out the Seminole athletic programs."

Payne recalled one particular incident shortly after he arrived in Sanford that was indicative of "Doc's" dedication to high school sports medicine.

"We were sitting in the stands one night watching a football game, and one of our players went down with an injury. It looked like a scene from the Keystone Cops. "Doc" goes charging out on the field with all his student trainers. They all wore these pouches on their belts that held medical instruments, tape, and supplies. Sometimes there were so many people working on one injured player it looked like a 30-second commercial for "The Bionic Man."

Then all joking aside, Payne turned serious for a moment.

"Looking back over the season, we've had the good fortune to be able to start the same five players for 30 games. Basketball is physical and demanding, and it's a tribute to "Doc's" efforts to keep everybody fit and in the lineup."

It seemed almost spooky that the two coaches, who would have so much on the line that Saturday night, would, out of the blue, bring up two issues that had not been part of any conversation through 30 games. Payne mentioned injuries, and Toth brought up finger-pointing or blame-fixing for a potential loss.

CHAPTER 20
Jubilant Redemption

Saturday morning, the eve of the District 9 championship game, had a little extra buzz to it.

I had just finished laying out my sports pages depicting Friday's semi-final games that advanced Mainland and Sanford to a decisive third encounter when the phone rang. It was my broadcasting counterpart Joe Johnson calling from WTRR.

"You think you might want to throw a set of headphones on and do color commentary tonight?" he asked.

"I don't know, Joe. I'll need to touch base with the boss. My newspaper and your radio station kind of compete for advertising dollars, so that might be a little problematic. Let me get back to you in a bit."

Although he didn't arrive at the crack of dawn on Saturday mornings, managing editor Tom Giordano was usually in the office around 8 a.m.—just about the time I sent my pages back to composition and headed to The Colonial Room for a customary weekend breakfast of scrambled eggs, grits, toast and a slice of country ham.

Giordano flagged me down as I headed out the door to eat.

"So, Seminole High and Mainland in the title game tonight?" as if he didn't know.

"That's the shape of things," I confirmed.

Then he smiled and gave me my marching orders.

"They've had a helluva season, Joe. So, win, lose, or draw tonight against Mainland we're going to want a Page 1 story as well as your game stories in the sports section."

"Not a problem I grinned," happy at the prospect of making it to Page 1 Above the Fold a second time that season.

Then I broached the subject of doing color commentary for WTRR.

At first, Giordano was hesitant, mentioning the very topic I suspected he would, competition for advertising dollars between the newspaper and radio station.

I put my salesmanship hat on and tossed him my pitch.

"Look, Tom, I understand the advertising concerns, but this is a really unique situation. I can go on air and be an ambassador for *The Sanford Herald*, and in a way, it's almost a public service. Mainland's gym is so small there's going to be half the Sanford community that wants to see the game, but only about 500 can get in. It's a win-win if I wear two hats tonight."

Giordano leaned back in his squeaky office chair, lit up another of his ever-present Marlboros, then a slow smile crept across his face.

"You know, that's a pretty slick argument for a sports guy," he chuckled.

"All right, you've got the green light to wear two hats tonight. Go ahead and do color for the radio station."

So, it was settled. I would dust off my broadcasting skills honed with Uncle Sam a few years earlier at Armed Forces Network-Europe and multitask.

By 9:40 that night, Joe Johnson had a broadcast partner, I had another Page 1 story, and Bill Payne and his Fighting Seminoles had an 800-pound gorilla lifted off their shoulders. The "Above the Fold story" double-deck headline screamed:

Triumphant Seminole Team Crows: 'What Do the Pollsters Say Now?'

Seminole High basketball coach Bill Payne's Fighting Seminoles did what many thought impossible Saturday night. In a pressure-packed thriller, the Tribe knocked off Daytona Mainland 68-67 to earn a trip to the state playoffs.

The victory was especially sweet for the Seminoles whose only two losses of the regular season came at the hands of the Bucca-neers.

Frustrated by a 20-point pounding at Mainland just days ago and shaken by a last-second win over Apopka in the opening game of the district tournament, the Tribe put it all together, including a sparkling performance from the bench for the victory.

The Tribe fell from the state prep poll and was told they wouldn't even make it out of their district.

Seniors Bruce McCray and Glenn Stambaugh saw to it that they did.

McCray turned in a 31-point game to go along with six rebounds, by far his best performance of the year against Mainland.

For the second time in the tournament, Stambaugh canned the winning shot to pull the Seminoles from behind and into the win-ner's circle.

There were other heroes too. David Thomas controlled the boards for 13 rebounds, and the man in the middle, Reggie Butler, grabbed nine, four of them coming in the critical final minutes.

A courageous Keith Whitney tried returning to the lineup twice after injuring his knee and managed to hit an important bucket. Sixth man Shun Thomas came off the bench to help in the backcourt while "Big Bird" Steve Grace and Willie White bailed the Tribe out of early foul trouble with fine reserve performances.

Seminole coach Payne threw something at the Buccaneers they hadn't seen all year long—the triangle-and-two defense.

It all boiled down to Seminole High's biggest victory of the year, vaulting them into regional competition against Ft. Pierce Central Tuesday night. Herald Sports Editor Joe DeSantis recaptures the emotional-filled victory beginning on Page 5A.

Big wins certainly deserved big ink. And the Seminole's win got plenty of play on *The Sanford Herald's* inside sports pages. The details of Saturday night's District Championship carried this story headline:

"How Sweet It Was for Tribe"

Rumors of Seminole High's death have been greatly exaggerated.

Bill Payne's Fighting Seminoles left behind the frustration of two regular season losses to Daytona Mainland and the chagrin of being dropped from the state's prep top 10 poll Saturday to beat the Buccaneers in the one game that counted. The District 9 championship game.

Behind a 31-point effort from Bruce McCray and the clutch shooting of Glenn Stambaugh, Seminole tripped the Buccaneers 68-67 in a wire-to-wire thriller before a jam-packed crowd on the Buc's home court. Something no other team had done this season.

"This had to be the biggest win in my life," said an emotional Bill

Payne in a tumultuous Tribe locker room.

Indeed, emotions ran high. When the final buzzer sounded there were tears of joy among Seminole's followers and tears of frustration in the Mainland stands.

Just days earlier Mainland had walloped Seminole by 20 points. The Tribe then had to scrap for its life to make it to the championship game.

"The defense was the difference," a happy Payne pointed out. Mainland coach Dick Toth agreed.

"They used a defense on us that we hadn't seen all year," explained the Bucs' coach.

"Of course, I'm disappointed. If Henry had hit the one-and-one, we would be going to Ft. Pierce. But give the credit to Seminole, they won the game. I hope they go all the way to the state—it would be good for them to represent the conference and the district."

"We kind of had a feeling they wouldn't be able to adjust to the triangle-and-two defense," explained Payne.

"Nobody used it on them this year. It cut off a lot of Henry's high passes to their big men under the boards."

The contest was never more than seven points wide throughout.

Mainland jumped out 11-8 in the first period by hitting its first five shots. A Glenn Stambaugh jumper late in the second quarter gave Seminole its first lead at 22-21. The Tribe and the Bucs matched bucket-for-bucket before Sam Henry hit a 20-footer to give Mainland the halftime lead at 39-38.

A seesaw third period and a hot four minutes into the final stanza pushed the Tribe to a six-point lead before Mainland battled back

170

to eventually take the lead at 67-66 with 1:05 left in the game, setting up the final frantic minute.

Buccaneer guard Sam Henry then missed the front end of a one-and-one situation which would have given Mainland a three-point lead.

After two Seminole turnovers, Mainland had possession for an in-bound play at midcourt with 25 seconds left in the contest. Mainland's Herb Harris attempted an inbounds pass but David Thomas, who snared 13 rebounds on the night to go along with Reggie Butler's nine, slapped the ball right back into the still-out-of-bounds Harris' hands and the Tribe took over possession.

Thomas then inbounded to Bruce McCray who hit Stambaugh with a pass at the top of the key. Stambaugh dribbled right, pulled up, and aimed a 24-footer at the goal. The shot hit nothing- but-net and Seminole took the lead with 19 seconds.

Mainland raced down the court with Henry firing a long jumper, he missed, the ball went out of bounds, and Seminole took possession with just one second left.

David Thomas, attempting an inbounds pass to kill the clock, threw the ball the length of the court and it went out of bounds and Mainland had one more shot with one second.

Henry lobbed the ball up high trying to go to Herb Harris for a last-second tip-in. Henry drew plenty of company and the ball was batted around until the final buzzer went off, sending Mainland away empty-handed at 29-2 and sending the Seminoles into re-gional play at 29-2 also.

"I'm sorry for Mainland," commented Payne afterward. "They are such a class team. But I'm happy for us. Our kids had something

to prove, and they all pulled together to do it."

It was an exhausting and exhilarating week of high school basketball. And the game story was accompanied by a sidebar column I wrote trying to put the entire Tribe season into an 18-column inch sidebar perspective. It carried the headline:

"A Show of Character"

Ecstatic Seminole High basketball fans who witnessed Saturday night's emotionally draining victory against the Mainland Buccaneers are probably still playing the game repeatedly in their heads.

To more than a casual observer, so many intricate intangibles came into play, none of which the least include the sometimes-overworked cliches like heart, character, and guts.

Bill Payne's kids displayed all these qualities and more Saturday evening.

Consider for a moment all the circumstances and events leading up to the all-or-nothing contest. In the first meeting between two of Florida's premier prep teams, it was Mainland scoring a 78-75 victory on the Seminoles' home court.

A game in which many roundball knowledgeable people thought the Seminoles had performed to the apex of their ability. The Tribe cruised through the remainder of the regular season until the rematch, on the last night of the regular season before the district tournament.

But in that undefeated stretch, something lacked. Quite possibly it was the loss of intensity. More likely it was the loss of killer instinct that separates good teams from exceptional ones. Nevertheless, the early-season big winning margins turned into less than comfortable deciding margins.

Then came the disastrous rematch on the Buc's home court. A 20-point victory in which Seminole was completely outplayed, out-hustled and outclassed. A game in which the Tribe, for the first time in the entire season, lost its composure as a team.

A second psychological blow came two days later when the Florida High School Basketball poll was released. The previously third-ranked Seminoles found themselves nowhere to be found on the list of the state's best.

Yet a third unnerving factor came into play on the second night of the district tournament, when, after rolling out to an early lead, the Seminoles almost took an early vacation until next year at the hands of Apopka, before Glenn Stambaugh's foul shots saved the day.

In the semi-final victory over Lake Howell, the Tribe looked better and smoother but still didn't look like they had enough to knock off Mainland.

Saturday night they answered a multitude of questions. Saturday night they found themselves again, and equally as important, found out more about themselves in the win over the Buccaneers.

The winning chemistry came not only from the starting five, who, except for Stambaugh went through a tough sophomore season together but from depth on the bench.

Speaking in technicalities, the Buccaneers are a better team on paper. In a pure talent sense probably by a 3-1-1 margin. The Mainland starting five had also been intact for the better part of three seasons or more.

But Mainland's season is over, the Seminoles play on when they face Ft. Pierce Tuesday night on the road in regional competition.

A win there takes them one more step. Whether they keep going in the competition and possibly win all the marbles, the looks on their faces Saturday night said the Mainland victory was the one they'd remember most about this season.

CHAPTER 21
Road Warriors

There would be no rest for the Sanford Seminoles. Having played three grueling games over three nights to claim the District 9 tournament championship, Bill Payne's Tribe would have a mere 72 hours to regroup, prepare, and hit the road for regional competition.

Odd numbered districts were determined to be road teams for the 1979-80 season, so Sanford's squad would load up early Tuesday morning, March 4 to make the 125-mile trek to Ft. Pierce, situated on the shores of St. Lucie County. The area was nicknamed the "Treasure Coast" after a Spanish treasure fleet that sunk off the coast there in 1715. Ft. Pierce was one of the oldest communities along the east coast of Florida, and the treasure Seminole High would be seeking was the Region 5-Class 4A basketball championship.

A very tall and very talented Ft. Pierce Central Cobra team stood in their way.

As Regional play began around the state that Tuesday night, in addition to the Seminoles traveling to Ft. Pierce, there was good basketball to be played up and down the state of Florida's 447-mile north-to-south geographical stretch. The slate of the state's other Regional games clearly illustrated that the road to Lakeland for Florida's Class 4-A Final Four would be a challenge. And without looking ahead, it was impossible for any teams still involved in post-season play not to eyeball potential opponents over the next week. Other Regional play that night would showcase:

Region 1: Pensacola Washington-vs-Ft. Walton Beach

Region 2: Jacksonville Ribault-vs-Jacksonville Englewood

Region 3: Orlando Evans-vs-Lakeland (There's that Metro Conference again).

Region 4: Tampa Robinson-vs-St. Pete Boca Ciega

Region 6: West Palm Beach Twin Lakes-vs Ft. Lauderdale Oakland Park NW

Region 7: Miramar-vs-Miami Carol City

Region 8: Miami Jackson-vs Miami Palmetto

Before heading south down Interstate, I-95, Payne talked about how difficult it was to prepare for an opponent the Tribe had never seen before. He shared some of the scouting reports he'd been able to assemble over the weekend and into Monday.

"They're a little bigger than us inside and at their guards," Payne informed.

"Ft. Pierce has a front line that measures 6-7 at the center, 6-4 and 6-5 at the forwards, and 6-0 and 6-3 at the guards."

Seminole would once again counter with the front line of 6-6 Reggie Butler in the pivot, and leaper David Thomas and scorer Bruce McCray at the forward positions, both hitting the measuring tape at 6-4.

Shooting ace Glenn Stambaugh would again be set to go at one guard position, while Payne was hopeful that speedy point guard Keith Whitney would be back in the lineup. It was almost ironic that just a few days earlier, Payne was reflecting on how well team trainer Jim "Doc" Terwilliger had been able to keep the Seminole's starting five injury-free and upright through a 31-game season, then Whitney banged up a knee in the do-or-die District title game against Daytona Mainland.

"I'd like to start the same five players we've started in all 31 games this year," said Payne.

"We'll have to wait until we get down there this evening to see how well Keith can run."

Although the Seminoles would be facing an opponent they hadn't seen that season, the coach made no special adjustments in that Monday's final practice session.

"We're 29-2, so we'll stay with the same things that got us here," he explained of his game plan for Ft. Pierce.

"Anytime you play somebody you haven't seen you have to go with your game plan to start with and then adjust to what the competition does."

Payne's defensive adjustment that past Saturday against Daytona Mainland proved to be the winning difference in the Seminole victory. The Tribe boss threw a strategy at the Buccaneers that they hadn't seen before—the triangle-and-two defense.

"Basically, it's a tight zone under the boards and one-on-one defense at the guards," he expounded.

"We thought about using it against Mainland in the second game, but we thought we would save it for the one game that counted," he smiled.

The Tribe would once again be counting on the inside scoring punch of Bruce McCray, who tallied 31 against Mainland in the District showdown, and the outside marksmanship of Glenn Stambaugh, who came up with a pair of game-winning tournament shots.

Repeated strong defensive and rebounding efforts would again be needed from Reggie Butler and David Thomas. And thinking ahead in light of Whitney's knee injury, Payne told me he would likely start his sixth man, Shun Thomas at the point if Whitney's wheels couldn't make it a go.

In the Mainland contest, Shun turned in a good night, feeding a hot shooting Stambaugh with multiple assists, while David Thomas and Reggie Butler both had huge nights in the District title game with 13 and nine rebounds, respectively.

"Their scoring is based on a two players attack," Payne shared.

"They have a 6-3 guard who is built like Quinn Buckner, and he's supposed to be a good penetrating guard. One of their forwards also plays a big role in the offense, so we'll have to play good defense in the backcourt and under the boards."

Payne added, "It's tough to play somebody you don't know much about, but they didn't get to be 28-3 and make it to the Regionals without being a very good basketball team."

Sanford radio station WTRR would once again broadcast the game with Joe Johnson on the call, a great benefit to the majority of the student body and Sanford community who couldn't make the long road trip on a school night set with an 8 p.m. tipoff.

"We want to get down there a little early, eat, and rest up before the game," Payne said of the Seminole's planned mid-day departure from Sanford.

Sam Cook and I would likewise depart early that afternoon and tag-team the game. Managing editor Tom Giordano once again wanted a Page 1 Above the Fold story to go along with features and sidebars for the inside sports pages.

As we were packing up notepads and scorebooks along with my trusty Asahi Pentax 35-millimeter camera and plenty of Tri-X Pan black and white film to hit the road, I stuck my head in his office and jokingly told him, "You know this is a 250-mile round trip. The sports department's been selling a lot of newspapers this season. I'm going to pad the hell out of my mileage reimbursement form."

Giordano busted out with a good belly laugh, lit up another of his ever-present Marlboro's then reached into his pocket.

He pulled out two crisp $20 bills and handed them to me.

"Here's a little meal money for you and Sam off the books. Bring us back some good stories."

It was about a two-and-a-half-hour ride to Ft. Pierce that afternoon and on the way down Sam and I kind of recapped what an eventful basketball season it had been. It turned into a memorable four-month journey not only for Seminole High but for all the teams in the Five Star Conference. And the season had given us both the opportunity to come to know both the coaches in the area we covered and their players as well. And we discussed how great it would be for Seminole County basketball to notch a state championship.

Then we also did a coin flip. Sam won and would write the Page 1 Above the Fold game story. I would handle inside-page feature material. By about 9:45 that night, we both had plenty to write about. Sam's Page 1 story carried the headline:

"Seminoles Dance into Final 8"

Seminole High School forward Bruce McCray turned snake-charmer in the final three minutes to uncoil Ft. Pierce Central's Cobras 68-

62 and give Sanford the Region 5-4A basketball championship Tuesday night at Ft. Pierce.

The Seminoles now travel to West Palm Beach Twin Lakes in a Sectional competition Saturday night. A victory there will send them to Lakeland as one of the Final Four teams in the Class 4-A tournament.

The 6-4 McCray turned on the charm with seven straight points to lift a stumbling Tribe from a 55-52 deficit to a 63-60 advantage in a furious two-minute span.

With the Cobras holding a 55-52 lead following a questionable technical, assessed of the Seminole players for getting back to the floor too slowly, McCray went to work.

First, 6-6 Reggie Butler picked off an errant pass and found quick Keith Whitney down the left sideline. Butler fed Whitney, who found McCray for a shot, but the big forward was fouled.

McCray banged home one free throw but missed the second leaving the score tied at 55 and only 2:40 left to play. On the missed free throw, Ft. Pierce tipped the ball out of bounds, but the Tribe failed to capitalize as guard Glenn Stambaugh missed a fadeaway jumper on the baseline.

After a timeout, the Cobras' 6-2 guard Luther Sandifer was slapped by Stambaugh on a jump shot. Sandifer converted the first free throw but missed the second.

A wild scramble ensued, and Wayne Titus threw in the rebound shot and was fouled by Stambaugh. Ft. Pierce led 58-55. Stambaugh's luck turned for the better, however, as Titus missed the free throw with 2:09 remaining.

"Titus has been our best free throw shooter all year long for us," a dejected Cobra coach Bill Wright said after the game. "He's by far our best free throw shooter. I thought we had them."

Despite Wright's thoughts, it turned out it was the Cobras that were being had. McCray quickly drained the Ft. Pierce venom with a six-point outburst.

First, he drew a foul and calmly sank two free throws to pull the Seminoles within 58-57. Wilbert Washington, who at one point was six-for-six in the ball game, fired from the baseline to make it 60-57.

McCray, undaunted, made a nice move across the lane for a bucket to pull the Tribe with one again at 60-59. Then Stambaugh corralled an important missed shot and found McCray at the other end of the court to give Sanford its first lead 61-60 since midway through the third quarter.

The Tribe press forced a turnover and Keith Whitney was fouled. The unflappable Whitney connected on both for a 63-60 edge with only 1:12 remaining.

"My knee still hurt but I had to get out there," said Whitney, who was termed questionable because of the injury suffered against Mainland.

Seconds later Whitney collided with Washington and was whistled for a foul. Washington however, feeling like a snake-bitten Cobra, caromed the free throw to an eager McCray. The agile senior took off on the dribble to half court where the now uncoiling Cobras attempted to double team. McCray alertly found a lonesome David Thomas underneath the basket for a widening 65-60 margin.

"My man picked up on Bruce which left me open," Thomas pointed out about his easy layup which seemed to make the Cobras un-ravel and shed their skins.

Down by five with 45 seconds to play, Central threw the ball out of bounds and with it any chances of a miracle opportunity.

"When we got down the kids sucked it up," coach Bill Payne said about the comeback.

"When Ft. Pierce got behind, they didn't have the heart to come back."

Stambaugh, who ignited an early uprising with six first-quarter points, agreed with his coach's assessment.

"We had the guts," said the Tribe's Medicine Man.

"We realized if we lost it would be our last game. We didn't have the intensity at the beginning of the game. We were so up for Mainland that it took a little while to get going in this game."

Another slow starter was Reggie Butler, who had more than his hands full battling 6-7 Mike Toomer, the 6-4 Washington, and 6-5 Curtis Redden, who is the brother of 6-11 Willie Redden, a for-mer Cobra All-Stater now at the University of South Florida.

"I was really surprised," said Butler about Central's leaping abil-ity.

"I wasn't mentally ready, but David and Glenn were slapping me upside the head to get me going."

McCray didn't need any head slapping to get him going. The smooth senior pumped in 13 first-half points, but Central still led at halftime 28-27 when Sandifer stole the ball and dunked it.

Sandifer also had 10 first-half points and turned in a good defen-sive job on Stambaugh after the 6-1 blond shooter burned him *early.*

Both teams employed man-to-man pressing defense which kept up the tempo throughout.

"I was a little worried about foul trouble," said Payne of his pressure defense.

"Thomas did get his third but that was the only problem. We did a good job of getting the ball to the guy who was hot," he emphasized.

Most of the time that was McCray, who paced the Seminole attack with 28 points. Stambaugh followed with 16 points including a couple of timely steals along with Thomas to recover from a 45-38 third-quarter deficit. Whitney contributed 12 while Thomas added 10.

For the losing Cobras, Toomer, who tried to put Sanford away with 10 points in the final quarter, finished with 16 points for the night. Washington also tallied 16 points, while Titus added 13 and Sandifer chipped in 11.

"Our press was the key and we played good defense," concluded Payne.

"We also appreciate the kids and the fans who made the trip. Sanford is behind us.

"We're one game away from Lakeland and we want it bad," said Payne about the now impending Saturday game in West Palm Beach against Twin Lakes, winners over Ft. Lauderdale Oakland Park.

"We can smell it."

No doubt the fragrance is pretty sweet.

One of the luxuries of having two sports writers at the same game is that one can focus on the game story itself, as Sam did, and the other can be more of a casual observer about the nuances and sidebar tidbits that go into a sporting event. Plus, my time in Army journalism school also came with some basic photography and darkroom training. So, it spared managing editor Tom Giordano having to send staff photographer Tommy Vincent or Tom Netzel along with us. Now, I certainly wasn't as good as *The Sanford Herald's* two Toms, but I knew enough to put film in the camera, take the lens cap off, and point the thing in the general direction of the subject matter. A few of the journalistic tidbits that added to the fabric of Seminole High's Road win over Ft. Pierce Central:

David Thomas on composure: "It comes from coach Payne yelling at us a lot," laughed Thomas, who battled the flu Tuesday night as well as the Cobras on the boards.

Glenn Stambaugh about keeping the team's head together late in pressure-packed games, especially when the Tribe was trailing late: "We're a team of seniors, and we all realize where we want to go and what we have to do to get there. We also know if we lose, we go home."

Then he added: "Maybe we don't play with intensity until the fourth quarter. Believe me. We don't plan on being behind."

An emotionally drained Reggie Butler: "This is the big time for me. We've never been this far before. And the Lord willing, we will make it to Lakeland. We want it bad."

Bruce McCray on the Tribe's late-game winning surges: "We try to keep our heads in the game, but we can't wait for the fourth quarter anymore."

Fancy meeting you here: On the long drive back home from Ft.

Pierce, a honking Buick pulled up alongside the Tribe's lead travel van, driven by coach Payne. The driver signaled for Payne to roll his window down. When he did, much to Payne's chagrin, he was greeted by the waiving officials who were supposed to have called the game. Somehow, they got bumped at the last minute, and instead, officials from Ft. Lauderdale were assigned to officiate the Region 5 contest. To the Seminole fans who made the lengthy road trip, it seemed the eleventh-hour Ft. Lauderdale zebras were good for about 10 points benefitting the Cobras.

The long and winding road: Fifty-five faithful Sanford followers were treated to a free chartered bus ride to the game by Kay Shoemaker of Shoemaker Construction in Sanford. The free-bee venture turned into a modern-day version of "Who's on First" when the first bus had to be replaced because it was emitting choking gas fumes. Not 30 miles north of Ft. Pierce on the return journey home, the second bus broke down on I-95. The weary travelers didn't make it back to Sanford until 4:30 Wednesday morning. Safe bet there were some students and fans late for school and work.

They're still growing boys: Helen Constantine and her Seminole High cafeteria crew made sure the Traveling Tribe was well fortified for their trip down and back. The staff prepared a seemingly endless supply of snacks for the Seminoles to munch on. Nonetheless, the Morrison's Cafeteria all-you-can-eat buffet in Vero Beach would never be the same after 14 hungry basketball players foraged for dinner when the team stopped for its 5 p.m. pregame meal.

You've got to face the music: Payne served as entertainment director on the ride down to Ft. Pierce, Or rather, entertainment dictator. He controlled the van's radio station selection and showed

185

a preference for Donna Summer and Neil Diamond. Center Reggie Butler did the coach one better on the late-night trek home. Shortly after the team had snuggled in for the return trip, the usually quiet Butler broke out with lead vocals on several current Top 40 hits. He got backup help from a chorus including Shun Thomas, "Big Bird" Steve Grace, Mike Gaudreau, and Robert Guy. No recording contract would be forthcoming for this group, however.

Take it for a test drive: Prior to the start of the Ft. Pierce game, Keith Whitney's knee injury left speculation that he might have to be sidelined against the Cobras. The speedy senior came out about 40 minutes prior to the start of the game to test his wheels. The noticeable limp from the Mainland game was gone, but he still wasn't 100 percent. "Keith hit some big shots for us in the fourth quarter and his shot selection was superb," complimented Payne. "He was really in control out there on the floor."

As David goes, so go the Seminoles: He doesn't necessarily score much and his game is sneakily deceptive, but when forward David Thomas is on, the whole squad is on. Thomas, the glue that held this team together and accountable all season long had a few words of praise for his frontcourt partner Reggie Butler, a little down at his third and early fourth-quarter rebounding performance. As a drained and disappointed Butler lingered in the locker room following the victory, Thomas stuck his head around the corner and told his fellow senior, "Hey Reg, you are number one, the best, man."

Touchy Technical: With four minutes remaining in the game and following a Bruce McCray bucket, a Ft. Pierce player went to inbounds the ball and then suddenly pulled up as if injured. The player seemingly signaled for a timeout and the Cobra's trainer and coach walked the length of the floor to check on him. The Seminoles went to their bench for a breather and were flagged for a technical foul. The referees would claim no timeout was called.

CHAPTER 22

Wednesday Morning Accolades

Following the Tuesday evening, March 4 win over Ft. Pierce Central, we rolled back into Sanford just as Tuesday night blended into Wednesday morning. There wasn't much time for more than a short nap before it was back to the office again to begin compiling pre-game information for feature pieces about the Tribe's next road game. The Sectional round of state playoffs would have them hitting the highway once more, this time for a Saturday night battle even further south down Interstate 95 to face West Palm Beach Twin Lakes.

But first, there was another story to be written. Seminole High's starting five woke up that Wednesday to a rarity. Here's how the news played out as the lead story on the sports pages of *The Sanford Herald* on March 5.

It's easy to understand why Bill Payne's Seminole High basketball team has enjoyed its great run this season. The starting lineup includes a nicely balanced mixture of scoring, defense, rebounding, and ball handling. Seminole County coaches think so too.

For their respective performances this season, the coaches have voted Seminole High's entire starting five to the yearly All-County team presented by Burger King.

The remaining five players on the 10-man squad include some pretty prime basketball talent also.

Figuratively speaking, the Tribe's starting five compiled the kind of numbers which clearly showed why they were the team to beat in the '79-80 season.

In the backcourt, there's sharp-shooting guard Glenn Stambaugh and the swift-footed Keith Whitney.

As a team, Seminole shot an amazing 57 percent from the floor during the regular season. Stambaugh contributed a 54-percent total of his own in averaging 11.2 points per game. The marksman also shot a blistering 89.9 percent from the charity stripe and dished out 92 assists. He also found time to scrape up 62 rebounds from his guard position.

Whitney was the man who made the running game go. The 5-10 sparkplug averaged just under 10 points per game with a 51-percent floor accuracy rate. More importantly, he led the team with a whopping 160 assists.

Many of his helping hand plays went to Bruce McCray, the squad's leading scorer.

McCray blistered the nets for a 66-percent mark from the floor averaging 21.6 points per game. When he wasn't hauling in a regular season team-leading 275 rebounds, he found time to break the school's single-season scoring record. The 6-4 point-maker also added 67 assists to his credit while shooting 67 percent from the free-throw line.

When it came to rebounding and defense, Payne looked to center Reggie Butler and forward David Thomas.

Butler averaged eight points per game and was the team's second-leading rebounder with 263. His 6-6 presence in the middle was also good for an average of four blocked shots per game.

Rounding out Seminole's All-County performers is 6-4 forward David Thomas. The man of a thousand moves snared 206 rebounds and averaged 10.6 points a game. He also handed out 106 assists and usually drew the opposition's toughest player to defend.

Lake Brantley's accurate guard Doug Dershimer capped his three-year career at the Big Blue campus by once again earning a spot on the All-County team. Post-season honors are nothing new to the "Bird Man." He was named to the Rotary Bowl All-Tourney team in '78 and '79 and the Oviedo-Outlook Invitational All-Tourney team both as a junior and senior. He was also selected Second Team All-Five Star Conference last season.

Dershimer led the Patriot offense with a 19.4 per game scoring average while shooting 49 percent from the floor.

The Orange Belt Conference Co-Champion Oviedo Lions placed their two talented seniors on the All-County squad.

For the second straight year, guard Troy Kessinger and wingman Horace Roland made the team.

Kessinger, who led the Lion football team to the Regional round of state playoffs at quarterback, averaged 13.8 markers a contest. The quick-handed six-footer palmed off 65 assists and came up with 76 steals while averaging a 43.4 field goal shooting percentage.

Roland picked up right where he left off a year ago, scoring and rebounding heavily for Digger Phillips' squad.

The 6-2 senior averaged 15 points on 48.9 percent shooting, hit 78.4 percent of his foul shots and snagged 137 rebounds. His speed also accounted for 34 assists and 53 steals on the year.

Lake Howell's "Mr. Offense" Reggie Barnes was selected to the All-County team for the second season running. The lightning-quick forward scored 501 points on the season, averaging 17.3 per game. He also played a big role on the boards, ripping 203 rebounds to average just over seven per game. The 6-2 senior found time to hand out 105 assists while shooting 79 percent from the free throw line and 49 percent from the floor.

Lyman Greyhound Neal Gillis rounds out the All-County team. Perhaps the most consistent player for the up-and-down squad of coach Tom Lawrence this season, Gillis, a junior, showed up every night to average double figures in both points and rebounds.

So as Seminole High was preparing for West Palm Beach Twin Lakes that week, Manny Garcia, the area's king of Burger King franchises, would once again be digging deep in his pockets to pony up for trophies and plaques to be presented later in March. And fittingly, the annual All-County awards banquet would be held at the very facility we used for our *Seminole Herald* mailbox Pony Express Pick Up spot--the Eastmont Civic Center at the city lines of Altamonte Springs and Longwood.

CHAPTER 23

Road Warriors 2.0

Tournament tested and showing increased roadworthiness; the Fighting Seminoles would pack their bags and pull out of Sanford at 1:30 on the afternoon of Saturday, March 8, for the trip to West Palm Beach. Waiting for them with home-court advantage would be a tall and talented Twin Lakes squad with eyes on the Section Championship and a ticket to the Class 4-A Final Four.

Twin Lakes had punched their ticket to the contest by beating Lake Worth Leonard 52-48 in their District Tournament and followed up with a 72-69 Regional win over Ft. Lauderdale Northeast. They matched up well under the boards against the Fighting Seminoles, and like Bill Payne's team, were battled tested in tight games.

Tribe center Reggie Butler had failed to score in the Regional win over Ft. Pierce Central and would now have to contend with West Palm's talented 6-7 junior Johnny Young in the paint. Butler promised a stronger game during practice leading up to the Sectional contest.

"I lost concentration at times because I was looking too much at the man with the ball and fell asleep on my man," explained the Tribe's soft-spoken pillar.

"I'm going to be better this time around."

Coaches often swap information with each other when facing competition they have never seen before, and in some cases, sports editors and writers do the same.

During the week I swapped notes on the respective starting lineups with Palm Beach Post prep sportswriter Dave George.

George gave me some insight into Twin Lakes forwards Dwayne Turner 6-7, and Tim Coney 6-4, both seniors. They would match up against the Tribe's David Thomas and Bruce McCray.

"Turner is not a classic power forward and prefers to take the outside shot from the baseline. He's considered a good leaper along with fellow forward Coney, the scavenger of the team," shared George.

George commented that, like the Tribe's Keith Whitney at the point, Twin Lakes had their "take charge quarterback" in 6-0 senior Johnny Peoples, considered a deadly outside shot who specialized in an up-tempo running jumper. Twin Lakes alternated two other players at the off-guard depending on whom they played and how the opposition matched up. Seminole High would get a dose of both Doug Wallace, a confident outside shooter against the zone, and lefty Eric Wilson, a sophomore who comes off the bench against man-to-man defenses.

The Palm Beach Post scribe also shared that Twin Lakes played best when they saddled up and ran the court. He told me Twin Lakes could run the other team right out of the gym when their outside shooting game was on and conversely, had a penchant for letting big leads slip away when forced to play at a slower pace.

Several of the Fighting Seminoles were battling a flu bug during the week's preparation for the Section game, and Payne knew they would also be challenged by a team with superior size.

"We're going to have to have a strong game under the boards against them," assessed Payne.

"And we have to play with more intensity right from the start," chipped in the Tribe's ace outside shot, Glenn Stambaugh.

"We can't afford to wait until the fourth quarter, not against this kind of competition."

While the Fighting Seminoles had been slow starters at times, they countered that with a sense of composure. Since the opening game of the District tournament, they had come from behind for three victories, including a pair of one-point wins not determined until the final seconds against Apopka and Daytona Beach Mainland.

"I think that's the sign of a good tournament team," observed Tribe assistant coach Tom Smith.

"So far, we've kind of been taking what the other teams give us and then taking it to them in the final minutes."

But Smith also pointed out that the Seminoles needed to find earlier intensity if they planned to make it to Lakeland, the site of the state's Final Four.

"Our running game has been hampered a little bit by turnovers, so we've slowed the pace down a bit. From here on in, we must play hard for four quarters."

Sitting just one game away from basketball's Holy Grail of the Final Four, the weight of the moment and perspective of the team's accomplishments to that point was beginning to register with both the players and their coach.

"This is the big time for us," acknowledged Butler.

"There's no turning back now," added Stambaugh, author of not one but two tournament-winning shots that had helped move the Tribe to lofty post-season heights.

During our pre-game preparation phone conversation, my sports writing counterpart Dave George added one more thought about the pending Saturday night clash between Sanford Seminole and West Palm Beach Twin Lakes.

"Everybody down in this neck of the woods was planning on having to play Daytona Mainland," he commented.

"Seminole High has really surprised a lot of people."

George was correct, and you could number the state prep pollsters among the surprised after they dropped Seminole High from the state's Top 10 poll following their second loss to Mainland.

According to them, the Seminoles should have packed their suitcases three games ago and called it a season.

But in winning more games than any other team in Seminole County history and advancing farther in post-season play than any other county team, Bill Payne and his Seminoles stand on the verge of reaping a three-year basketball harvest.

And Payne paused during this week's preparation for West Palm Beach Twin Lakes to put the season's accomplishments into perspective.

"These are great kids, great young people, not just great basketball players," complimented the Tribe coach.

"They have worked so hard for the past three years to get here."

His high-energy point guard, Keith Whitney, hasn't been shy about where the team stands at the moment.

"We want it all now," offered Whitney, who rebounded from a knee injury in the final Mainland game to resume his quarterbacking duties at point guard.

195

The Sanford community wanted it all as well.

"It's been phenomenal the reaction in the community as the season progressed," pointed out Payne.

"It's gotten to the point where if you go out in public everybody knows your face and offers good wishes."

Good wishes weren't the only thing the community was offering.

Payne laughed that there was a time or two when he took his kids to McDonald's for a weekend lunch, and the manager wanted to serve the family free food.

"I said no, if you don't let me pay for my family's food, I'm not coming back," he laughed.

There's an old saying in the military that an Army marches on its stomach.

And that was evident with the support from local businesses the Fighting Seminoles received.

Prior to their trip to Ft. Pierce Central for the Regional game, the local Western Sizzlin' in Sanford had sent the team off with a complimentary team meal.

And prior to their departure for West Palm Beach, Bill Painter, long-time proprietor of The Colonial Room Restaurant on East 1st Street, would section off the back room of the establishment and host the team for a meal to send them south with a home-cooked lunch.

And for those who could not make the long trip to West Palm, Sanford radio station WTRR would once again step up with help from local advertisers to install broadcast phone lines and send the game back to the hometown with an 8 p.m., broadcast with the familiar voice of preacher-by-day, broadcaster by night Joe Johnson behind the microphone.

CHAPTER 24

Lace Up Those Nikes

There are exactly 184.5 miles between Sanford and West Palm Beach. And as the crow flies south down I-95, it takes exactly two hours and 51 minutes to get from one location to the other. It would not only be a long ride for the Fighting Seminoles, but thanks to a pre-season promise he made to his team, a very expensive one for Tribe coach Bill Payne.

As my third Page 1 Above the Fold story headline in *The Sanford Herald* would explain, Seminole High would have another game to prepare for, and Bill Payne would have to go shopping.

On To Lakeland: Seminoles Aim to Win It All

They've traveled farther than any other team involved in the playoffs, and now Seminole High's Fighting Tribe roundball squad stands on the verge of bringing home its first-ever state basketball crown.

Bill Payne's troops once again dug deep Saturday night to handle West Palm Beach Twin Lakes for a 68-58 Section 3 win and a trip to Lakeland.

Now it's time for Payne to dig deep, as his players were so quick to remind him minutes after the victory that earned the Seminoles a berth as a Final Four squad in quest of the 4-A title.

"This one is going to cost me about 400 bucks," smiled the victorious coach.

"I told the team at the beginning of the season if they got me to Lakeland, I'd get them new Nike basketball shoes."

Maybe Payne can pick up some extra cash by pawning off the state tournament tickets that have been nestled in his wallet for some time now. He won't need them like any other spectator. His Seminoles have seen to it that the Tribe boss will be at courtside Friday night in Lakeland. He'll be trying to coach the Seminoles to their 32nd win of the year against Tampa Robinson, upset winners in overtime against season-long top-ranked Lakeland High.

"I'm going to give these to my wife and family," Payne said as he examined the state tournament entrance passes.

The road to Lakeland has been anything but easy or comfortable for the Seminoles.

"We had to travel farther than any other team involved in the playoffs," pointed out Payne of the Seminoles' long and cramped bus journeys to Ft. Pierce Central and West Palm Beach for Regional and Sectional victories.

"Going to Lakeland is one trip we won't mind at all. It will be like riding around the block."

Saturday's bus journey to West Palm Beach sounded like a trip from the hospital to the morgue.

Several of the Seminoles have been fighting the flu and Bruce McCray was battling a case of bronchitis. Reggie Butler was dealing with a smashed lip suffered in a final practice session.

"We kind of coughed and wheezed our way through this one," assessed Payne, equally drained by the flu.

"Maybe that story last week about us being so healthy all year was a jinx."

Maybe Seminole High principal Don Reynolds possesses powers to see into the future. A happy Reynolds hopped on the team bus shortly before the journey back home to Sanford to congratulate the Tribe and remind them it was time to break out something he'd given them about halfway through the season.

"Take out the bumper stickers," chuckled Reynolds to the team. "We're going to Lakeland.

"I gave the kids some bumper stickers that say "Lakeland-1980 State Basketball Tournament," earlier this year explained Reynolds.

"Now it's time to take them out and put them on."

"We really need the whole community down there for the state tournament," Payne exhorted. The place is huge and noisy. We really need all of Sanford's voices behind us."

If the Seminoles win Friday night against Tampa Robinson they will play the winner of the Pensacola Washington-Miami Palmetto semifinal.

Despite the flu bug and a tight game at the half, our inside sports page game story in *The Sanford Herald* illustrated that the Seminoles took control of the game early in the third quarter and finished off what could have been termed their most "comfortable" post-season win thus far.

Tribe Trips Twin Lakes for Section 3

Seminole High's 68-58 victory over West Palm Beach Twin Lakes Saturday night proved to be pretty expensive for Tribe coach Bill Payne.

The win, for the Section 3 championship and a shot at a 4-A state title, stands to cost the coach in the neighborhood of $400.

"I told them at the beginning of the season if they got me to Lake-land, I'd get them all new 'Nike" basketball shoes," explained a happy Payne in an equally happy locker room.

"I guess it's time to go shopping."

Payne's Seminoles did a little shoe-shuffling of their own Satur-day. Following a long bus ride, the Tribe stretched their legs, then stretched a 10-2 first-quarter lead into an almost comfortable full-game control.

Quite a change from the Tribe's last-minute antics that have car-ried them to the doorsteps of Seminole High's first-ever state bas-ketball championship.

The hot outside shooting of Glenn Stambaugh and the inside game of David Thomas staked the Seminoles to a 16-13 first-quarter ad-vantage, a spread they maintained at the half for a 27-24 margin.

The second quarter belonged to a less-than-healthy Bruce McCray, battling bronchitis as well as West Palm's 6-7, 6-7, 6-4 front line.

McCray followed up a four-point first-quarter effort with 11 in stanza two to offset the torrid display of Twin Lakes guard Tim Coney and strong inside play on the boards by West Palm.

Following a little locker room tongue-lashing at intermission, 6-6 senior center Reggie Butler came alive with two third-quarter open-ing buckets to push Seminole in front by seven. Butler's freshly in-spired play, along with David Thomas' bigger-than-life rebounding efforts against the taller West Palm Beach front line allowed Twin Lakes no closer than five points for the remainder of the game.

McCray equaled his 15-point first half with 15 more in quarters three and four to neutralize Coney's clutch shooting, but Semi-nole's balance proved too much for the taller Rams.

201

"They aren't what you would call real big, probably average team size," pointed out Twin Lakes coach Alvin Wright.

"But Seminole can jump. They took it to us on the boards."

And how far does the convinced Wright feel the high jumping Tribe can go?

"If they continue to play as they played against us, they can go all the way. They can beat anybody."

Payne will settle for a shorter outing to Lakeland, considering the distance his team has had to travel in beating both Ft. Pierce Central and West Palm beach on the road.

"I guess I won't need these," smiled Payne, holding tickets he had purchased for the state tournament weeks ago.

"Now my wife and some of my family can see the tournament."

Thomas, who ripped a game-high 14 rebounds to go along with Reggie Butler's 11 boards and 13 points nicely complimented a few well-placed Keith Whitney jumpers to round out the Seminole scoring. Whitney finished with 11 points while fellow guard Glenn Stambaugh chipped in with six to go along with a few nifty assists.

Coney paced the Rams with 17 to go along with forward Dwayne Turner's 17 and Doug Wallace's 13.

"I feel good. We're right where we want to be," commented a grinning Tribe assistant coach Tom Smith.

"Just two more games, we want to win two more," added Payne.

CHAPTER 25

Ink In 50-Gallon Barrels

There wasn't much that escaped the attention of *The Sanford Herald's* managing editor Tom Giordano, and he was fully cognizant of the post-season steps the Fighting Seminoles made since capturing the District 9 championship.

Giordano had been huddling with publisher Wayne Doyle and the advertising department with plans to boost readership, revenue, and good public relations in the community as the newspaper's coverage of the team played out.

Each Friday the publication had an eight-page tabloid supplement that normally featured entertainment information, highlights of television programming, movie releases, and the arts and culture scene in Seminole County. But things would be different for the March 14 issue of *The Sanford Herald's* "Leisure" tabloid.

It would be all sports. It would be all about Seminole High's march toward a possible state basketball championship. That also meant that in addition to our regular sports pages, my department would be responsible for filling the content of an additional eight pages of the tabloid that would come out the afternoon of that night's 8:30 p.m. tipoff in Lakeland between Seminole High and Tampa Robinson.

We would have to hustle to develop content to fill the space, which was easily a cash cow for the newspaper because multitudes of local businesses were eager to advertise in the tabloid in support of the team.

Eight pages is a lot of content; the sports department would need a 50-gallon barrel of ink to pull it off. But hustle we did. Giordano had advised me of the plan to turn the "Leisure" tabloid into a basketball special a few days before the West Palm Beach Twin Lakes game. If Seminole made it to the Lakeland Final Four the plan was a go. If Seminole had been eliminated by Twin Lakes, "Leisure" would feature its regular editorial content.

The center of an eight-page tabloid is known as a double truck when a story is spread out over the two inside middle pages. I had in mind a feature piece that would recap the entire season to fill that space.

And on the long, dark ride back home to Sanford from West Palm Beach, there was just enough light in the bus for me to take notes. Payne was tired and fighting the flu himself but was more than happy to talk about the team's journey that had begun nearly five months ago. We filled part of that satisfying trek home to Sanford with a lengthy conversation that became the feature piece of the "Leisure" tabloid. It carried the headline:

Chief Sitting Bill - The Man Behind the Miracle

The bags under his eyes are a little deeper and more noticeable in the past two weeks and his voice is sometimes raspy. But Seminole High basketball coach Bill Payne couldn't be happier. The long hours, weeks, months and three seasons that have consumed his efforts and energies stand on the verge of paying big dividends.

Bill Payne's Fighting Seminoles are knocking on the door of Sanford's first-ever state basketball championship.

"Sanford is on the map," he states emphatically about the Tribe's 1979-80 basketball prowess.

Indeed, the Seminoles have forced Florida to take notice. Owners of a sparkling 31-2 record that includes the District 9, Region 5, and Section 3 championships, the Seminoles are two games from reaching a goal thousands of prep cagers began thinking about months ago.

"I guess every player on every team has dreams about winning a state championship when practice starts," a drained but inwardly pleased Payne discussed during the long ride back from West Palm Beach following Seminole's 68-58 win over Twin Lakes that boosted them into tonight's semi-final contest against Tampa Robinson.

"Our dream can come true if we win two more games. Just two more games."

When the tall, curly-haired basketball boss arrived on the Seminole roundball scene three short seasons ago, the future looked like anything but a journey to Lakeland for the state championship tournament.

But patience, diligence, basketball smarts, and savvy coaching have paid off. Not overnight, but throughout the three seasons.

"These kids have really hung together and grown together," Payne compliments about his nucleus that took their lumps as sophomores, then improved to 14-11 as juniors. And this season's senior-laden squad has matured under his guiding hand to rebound from a variety of adversities.

"We were kind of sailing right along until that first meeting with Mainland," Payne reflected on his squad's first setback.

It came before a packed and partisan home crowd. His Seminoles battled the mighty Buccaneers down to the wire before bowing out 78-75.

205

"That loss was hard for the kids. They worked so hard for that game but came up a little short."

The Seminoles may have been a little short on that evening, but their character and Payne's coaching set them sailing on another winning streak. One that included victories both at home and on the road against three of the semi-finalists in the Metro Conference tournament.

"That's one of the reasons we're going to Lakeland," points out the former prep and college basketball sensation.

"We knew that if we wanted to find out how good we are, to see if we could get this far, we had to play an aggressive schedule."

According to Payne, that aggressive scheduling provided his Tribe with plenty of fine-tuning.

"When you go into snake pits like Evans and Boone and Colonial and beat them at their places and their style of game, it's got to help you," he assessed of the basketball showdowns with the Metro Conference teams.

"I owe a big round of thanks to a few of those Metro coaches, too," informs the Seminole boss.

"Guys like Dick Hulette at Evans and the coaching staffs at Oak Ridge and Boone and Colonial personally helped me prepare for West Palm Beach.

"Dick Hulette made available some videotape of the Rams and I got helpful information from the other coaches. That says a lot about the coaching profession when guys in your backyard are willing to help you out like that. I'm grateful to them."

Despite some wide-wining margins here in Seminole County, Payne feels the competition right in the Five Star Conference also pro-vided the Seminoles with a healthy testing ground.

"I was scared to death to play Lake Howell. Look back at those ball games. Every time we faced them, they were sky high for us and gave us fits.

"Lake Brantley almost knocked us off in the Outlook Invitational too," he reminded of the Tribe's slim 45-42 win over the Patriots.

Despite the tough neighborhood competition, his Seminoles seemed to be able to come up with whatever was necessary to win and continued to do so until the fatal final regular season rematch with Mainland's Buccaneers. This time on the opposition's home court.

For the first time, all season the Seminoles were out-played, out-hustled, and out-classed. For the first time, all season the Semi-noles lost their composure in an 80-60 debacle.

Had the Seminoles peaked emotionally in their first spirited effort against the Buccaneers?

"No," denies Payne flatly.

"I don't believe in that peaking business. They played better than us and they beat us."

The lopsided loss to Mainland couldn't have come at a worse time in the eyes of many Seminole followers. The District tournament was less than a week away.

But for Payne and the Seminoles, the spanking at the hands of the Daytona Mainland crew and the ensuing slap in the face by the prep pollsters may not have come at a better time. Two days after the loss the new prep Top 10 poll was released and much to the surprise and chagrin of the Seminoles and their fans, the Tribe had dropped from number three off the face of the Earth.

Why? Perhaps Paul Roche of the St. Petersburg Times and the co-ordinator of the poll summed it up best.

"They won't even make it out of their District," was how he commented on the Seminoles chances for post-season play.

Mainland coach Dick Toth added fuel to Payne's psychological fire by stating, "We beat them at their place, and we beat them at home. I think that should prove something. We don't like anybody coming in here and showing us how to play."

How did Payne feel his Seminoles would perform in the District tournament following the back-to-back psychological blows?

"I honestly had no idea how we would perform after the second loss to Mainland," recalled Payne.

"Reporters kept asking me and asking me about the District tournament and I didn't know what to tell them. I had no idea of how we would play after the second loss to Mainland."

Payne's troops hardly gave their head man a strong ballot of confidence when it took a couple of last- second free throws by Glenn Stambaugh to squeeze the Tribe past Apopka in the first round. Then the Seminoles had to face season-long nemesis Lake Howell in the District semi-finals.

Although they looked better, a cloud of uncertainty hung over the Tribe as it prepared for the third and decisive clash with Mainland, this time with the District title and a state playoff berth at stake.

"The triangle-and-two defense was the key," explained Payne of the Seminoles' triumph by a single point in the one game that

counted.

"I used all the bad news, all the negative things people said about us to fire the kids up again. They reached deep for that game. They wanted it more than Mainland."

And how much do Payne and his squad want the state championship?

"We've worked hard for the last three years. We think we have a good team and good kids.

"Just two more games. We want to win two more."

While earlier in the season Sam Cook had to pry predictions about the outcome of Seminole High's matchups against Mainland with a crowbar from Payne's Seminole County coaching counterparts, there was a growing sense of confidence about the Tribe's chances the further they advanced in state playoff action.

Young Benton Wood revisited several Five Star coaching rivals and a few of the players who faced Seminole along the way to measure their collective outlooks about a possible state title game for the Tribe.

His story was a natural element to include in the "Leisure" supplement and carried the headline:

It's a Consensus Opinion - They Can Win It All

As this year's state high school basketball tournament quickly approaches, many of us pull our crystal ball out of the closet and make like Jimmy the Greek.

But who would have believed at the beginning of the roundball season that the Seminoles of Sanford would still be alive and kicking in the final four of the state tournament?

"We lost to one of the best teams in the state," replied Lyman coach Tom Lawrence after his Greyhounds lost to Sanford in the finals of the Rotary Bowl Classic to start the season. *"Seminole will be tough to beat in this district."*

Maybe Lawrence should take up fortune-telling. Not only did Sanford win the District title, but they have advanced all the way to Lakeland for the state semi-finals Friday evening against Tampa Robinson.

Lawrence was right a second time around when he picked Sanford to beat Mainland in the district final.

"I really thought that if Mainland beat Sanford both times during the regular season, that they (Seminole) would come back and win it the third time around."

Well, as long as he's picked two in a row, let's see what his forecast is this time.

"They definitely have a good shot at winning it all," observed the second-year Lyman head coach.

"They have an excellent rebounding team, they shoot well, and play stiff defensive ball...that's what you need to win a state title.

"I'm all for 'em. It would be a big thing for basketball in the Five Star Conference to have a state championship. I know there are plenty of coaches around the state who would like to be in the same position as coach Payne is in now."

Lake Brantley coach Bob Peterson's job wasn't made easy for him as his Patriots ran into the awesome task of facing Seminole four *times this season.*

"Sanford's five positions are well-filled, and it will take a really tall or a very quick team to beat them," commented the Patriot's court general.

Peterson cites forward David Thomas as the key to the Seminole's success.

"Thomas has been playing really well lately. He will have to come through again if Sanford is to have a chance at it.

"Having played away from home will be a big plus for Sanford," added Peterson. He was referring to the Seminoles District win at Daytona Beach Mainland followed by the Sectional victory at Ft. Pierce and the Regional win at West Palm Beach.

Lake Howell coach Greg Robinson also had his troops face Sanford four times this season, only to leave empty-handed in each case.

"I like their chances," said Robinson of the Seminoles.

"They've learned to play tempo basketball and it has helped them a lot."

Interestingly enough, Robinson contradicts Peterson in that he feels Sanford's success is determined by the Seminole guards, Keith Whitney and Glenn Stambaugh.

"Stambaugh has done a super job for them," said Robinson.

"Teams try to stack up against them inside but then Stambaugh will hurt you from the outside. Once he hits a few shots, it opens things up for Whitney to penetrate and for the big men inside. I felt all along that both Mainland and Sanford had the material to go to the state tournament."

Robinson hinted that Sanford has gotten by their toughest test

211

when they beat Mainland in the district final.

"If they can control the tempo, they'll be tough to beat. This will be a true test for Sanford. Hopefully, they can bring home the state crown to Seminole County."

Let's hear from the folks who had to tangle with the Seminoles on the court this year.

"I knew they were going to be good when the season started, But I wouldn't have believed they would go to state," said Lyman senior center Glynn Bailey.

"They have a good coaching staff, and they play well together. I hope they win it all."

"Sanford has an excellent shot at it now," concluded Lake Brantley's All-Conference guard Doug "The Bird Man" Dershimer.

"Once you get this far all it takes is a few breaks to win it all. Stambaugh and McCray are two of the finest players around and they'll give a few people fits down in Lakeland."

"They're going to win the state title," predicted Greyhound guard Sam Lemon confidently.

"They've got things going pretty good now and I don't think anyone can stop them."

To the untrained eye and those unfamiliar with high school campuses, when it comes to supporting athletics and extracurricular activities, there are normally two types of high school principals. Those who wholeheartedly embrace sports, clubs, and other non-academic functions and throw a principal's weight fully behind them. Then there are those principals who tend to keep things at arm's length and just see athletics and extracurriculars as other activities that demand additional resources.

For those familiar with the daily ebb and flow on the Seminole High campus, principal Don Reynolds fell fully in the camp of gung-ho support. And he set the tone for universally embracing what the basketball team had done and meant to the student body, faculty, and entire Sanford Community as their season progressed.

Sam Cook captured his thoughts about the Fighting Seminoles in another feature piece for that Friday's "Leisure" supplement to *The Sanford Herald*. Those sentiments were reflected in his sidebar story that carried the headline:

Reynolds: "They've Brought Happiness and Harmony"

If Seminole High School Principal Don Reynolds could have his way---he'd prescribe a state-contending basketball team every year for his high school.

The personable Reynolds maintains the Tribe's impressive 31-2 slate going into the state tournament this Friday in Lakeland has been just the tonic to keep his school on an even keel.

And as everybody knows happy students go a long way in making an administrator's job that much easier.

"It's one of the best things that's ever happened to the school," Reynolds pointed out Tuesday evening.

"It's pulled the student body together behind the team.

"When you're walking the halls, the place seems a little more alive. Everybody talks about the team and the game coming up. It's a vibrant feeling."

*Reynolds also points to a feeling of pride which he thinks was ini-
tiated by the team and that has carried over to the students.*

*"I think it has established pride in the student body too. Every-
body's going around saying Seminole is number one and usually
this time of year there's nothing going on. Of course, that pride
started with the basketball team itself," reminded Reynolds.*

*It was a pride that was established early. The Fighting Seminoles
ran off 17 straight victories on their way to a number three state
ranking.*

*Included in the string were tournament championships in the Ro-
tary Bowl Tournament and the Oviedo-Outlook Christmas Tournament.*

*Then the first setback came. Daytona Mainland, unbeaten and
ranked second in the state at the time, edged Seminole 78-75 in
a game that was decided in the final seconds.*

*There were no reported suicides in the clinic the following Mon-
day though.*

*"No, that one didn't bother the students too much," confirmed
Reynolds.*

*"They knew Mainland was a great team and after all, they were
ranked ahead of us."*

*After the Mainland loss, coach Bill Payne's Tribe remained un-
beaten until a return encounter with the Bucs—this time in Daytona Beach.*

*"The 20-point loss hurt," remembers Reynolds about Sanford's
second loss.*

"It lowered our expectations. The students were not negative, they

realized Mainland was superb, but that game really hurt."

The next tumble didn't come on the court but off. St. Petersburg Times sportswriter Paul Roach coordinates the weekly poll for the rankings.

When the poll came over the United Press International wire service, the Sanford squad had not only fallen out of the top 10 but also out of the poll entirely. Two losses to the second-best team in the state and all of a sudden you don't rate.

Upon prompting by Sentinel Star Prep Sports Editor Frank Carroll, Roach rechecked his rankings and somehow found there was an oversight (no, not that he still had a job)—the Seminoles WERE in the category "also receiving votes."

What probably happened was, as a face-saving move, Roach inserted the Seminoles to appease the outraged cries of the Sanford faithful.

"Ten people must have told me they called St. Pete," Reynolds relates about the snub.

"We were mad as a wet hen. But we realized were we a small school in a small town."

Roach defended his dumping by saying the Seminoles weren't going to win their district, so they didn't deserve to be in the Top 10. And all this time you thought he was ranking the best teams in the state and not potential district champs.

Anyway, Sanford upset Roach, the poll, and Mainland when guard Glenn Stambaugh turned hero for the second night in a row as the Tribe edged the Bucs 68-67. Forward Bruce McCray with 31 points carried Sanford most of the night until Stambaugh's jump shot reverberated off downtown St. Pete.

"We got them (Mainland) when it counted the most," Reynolds said about the dramatic District tourney win.

"I've never been in a situation when I've seen so many people so happy. It was complete elation. Everybody I would see—the basketball team was all they would talk about."

Now if you think McCray, Stambaugh, Reggie Butler, Keith Whitney, and David Thomas are ready for the priesthood—Reynolds says maybe not just yet.

"You know, not all of these guys are angels," cautions Reynolds.

"Coach Payne's become very attached to this wild crew. It hasn't been easy. They wouldn't have come this far without excellent coaching. Bill's a scholar of this game. He's excellent at switching defenses.

"And more than that he's a tremendous motivator. He's brought in so many new improvements that it's been unbelievable," exclaimed Reynolds.

Along with Payne's on and off-the-court motivation, Reynolds likes to point a finger toward assistant principal Lamar Richardson and his "counseling" services.

"Some of these players are like Mr. Richardson's sons" informed Reynolds.

"He advises them and talks to them every day. I don't think he's missed a game either."

Richardson is given credit for turning around McCray's career in a closed-door meeting during the Tribe's leading scorer's sophomore year.

"There is a tendency to give me all the credit because I'm the disciplinarian but that's not true," Richardson modestly related.

"Wayne Epps (assistant principal), Cornelius Franklin (Dean), Jay Stokes (attendance), and myself all work together. It's a team effort.

"The thing I'm most pleased about is how these boys have been able to handle success when most of them haven't been successful before," said Richardson of the same cast that won only a few games as sophomores.

Sanford's success notwithstanding, just how far can the Seminoles go?

"Well, we hope all the way," laughed Reynolds.

"To me, the hardest part will be Friday. But if they win then, the hardest game will be Saturday. As far as I'm concerned, they're champions if they don't win another game."

Reynolds went on to say that it's been a unique team in more ways than its awesome record.

"It's a team that everyone cares for. When a player needed some shoes, I went out and bought him some shoes," said Reynolds. "We take care of them."

Along with taking care of the players, Seminole High is taking care of the fans.

"The high school went up and bought 500 tickets and brought them back to the school," said Reynolds.

"We want to take 1,000 people from Sanford."

Now if the Seminoles can just take care of two more opponents.

CHAPTER 26

Scouting Reports, Records, and Dark Clouds

The final pre-game feature piece that would complete the basketball-themed "Leisure" supplement in *The Sanford Herald* would be a scouting report on the potential matchups between the Fighting Seminoles and their state semi-final opponents, the Tampa Robinson Knights. My story was put to "bed" Thursday morning, a full day before the 8:30 Friday night tip-off.

Tribe coach Bill Payne minced no words about the information he'd been able to gather in his pre-game preparation. And he outlined the obstacles Tampa Robinson presented in Seminole High's path to a potential state championship game Saturday.

His assessment was direct in the advanced story that carried the headline:

Seminoles Set Sights on Tampa Robinson

"They are simply devastating inside," shared Payne of the Knight's bread and butter game plan at the forwards and at the center.

"They just take it to you and try to jam it inside."

Size-wise, the Seminoles match up against Tampa Robinson almost inch-for-inch.

Starting at the pivot for the Knights will be 6-6 Sylvester James, a senior who owns a 21-point-per-game average. He'll match up against Seminole's 6-6 Reggie Butler. Butler carries only a seven-point-and-change average on offense. More important, will be how well Butler can defend the high-scoring Knight center.

218

Tampa Robinson's offensive punch is rounded out at the forwards. Starting for the Knights will be 6-5 junior Charlie Bradley and 6-3 senior John Brumfield.

Bradley owns a healthy average at 20.8 points per game while Brumfield holds an 11.8 average. Both are considered superior jumpers along with center James.

Bill Payne will once again counter with the front line of 6-4 David Thomas and 6-4 Bruce McCray.

McCray has boosted a regular season scoring average of 21.9 points up to better than 28 points a contest in playoff action. The Tribe will need every bit of David Thomas' fine rebounding efforts in post-season play also.

Against a taller West Palm Beach Twin Lakes squad, Thomas ripped down a game-high 14 rebounds, undaunted by the Ram front line of 6-6, 6-6, and 6-6.

A key to a Seminole victory may well rest in the play of the back-court.

If Thomas, Butler, and McCray can play the Knights to a standstill under the boards, Seminole has the edge.

Starting for Tampa Robinson at guards will be 6-0 senior Dick Lovett and 5-11 senior Tim Wheless.

Lovett carries a seven-point average, and Wheless is averaging eight points per game. But in their Sectional win over Lakeland, both Knight guards were held scoreless.

Matching up against them will be the familiar faces of 5-10 Keith Whitney and 6-1 Glenn Stambaugh.

If Stambaugh and Whitney can connect from the outside, their shooting could be the deciding factor in whether Seminole plays Saturday night. However, Payne feels the key is the inside game.

"Most people think you should hit from the outside to open things under the boards," points out the Seminole coach.

"I'm just the opposite. I think if we can challenge them inside it will open things up for Keith and Glenn."

Strength-wise the Seminoles appear to have the better bench and they've gone to it with success throughout the season and into the playoffs.

Sixth man Shun Thomas may well be the best sixth player at the state tournament, capable of spelling either Stambaugh or Whitney at guard.

If Payne needs reserve strength under the boards he'll turn to Steve Grace at the center and Willie White at forward.

According to scouting reports, Tampa Robinson's strength in reserve is in backup guards Kenny Gunn and Darryl Patterson. Gunn is an excellent defensive player while Patterson, a fellow junior, possesses a good outside shot and came off the bench to score 12 against Lakeland.

The Seminoles will be a lot healthier for tonight's game than they've been in the last two weeks. The Tribe has had to survive a team bout with the flu in addition to some pretty sound competition in making it to the semi-final game in Lakeland.

A victory tonight sends them against Pensacola Washington for the 4A state championship, a first for a Seminole High basketball team.

"We've worked hard for the last three years to get where we are," *concluded Five Star Conference Coach of the Year Payne.*

"A win Friday night puts us where we want to be. But we can't even think about Saturday yet. Tampa Robinson is an awesome team. It will take a great effort to beat them.

"We'd like everybody to wear our school color orange tonight," added Payne.

"We want to let them know we're all from Sanford."

Sanford radio station WTRR will broadcast the Seminole-Tampa Robinson encounter beginning at 8:15 p.m. with the pre-game show.

The final piece of our eight-page "Leisure" supplement would be a check on the team and school records the Fighting Seminoles had either tied or beaten during their '79-80 run, which meant one final huddle and consultation with Seminole High team statistician Dean Smith. After crunching the numbers his '79-80 season statistics indicated new school records in several categories:

*Most points for a season at 2,276, breaking the old 1972 record of 1,936.

*Most points in a single game (97 twice)-tied record of 97 set in 1959 and matched in 1977.

*Most rebounds in a season (1,207), smashing the 1972 record of 975.

*Most rebounds in a game (51), breaking the 1972 record of 45.

*Best offensive average at 68.9 points per game, beating the 1968 record of 67.7 points per game.

*Highest field goal percentage (57), beating the 1970 school record of 54 percent.

221

*Most wins in a season (31), obliterating the 1972 record of 21 victories.

*Best season record (31-2) beating the 1972 record of 21-7.

The eight-page supplement would be completed with a generous sprinkling of photographs our ace shooters Tommy Vincent and Tom Netzel had compiled throughout the season.

Seminole High was indeed packing an impressive resume for its Friday trip to Lakeland. But basketball fortunes can be fateful and fickle. Much would take place between the time press manager Frank Voltoline hit the green power button Thursday to run the "Leisure" section for advanced packaging in the Friday newspaper.

And it almost seemed hauntingly ironic that our final stories talked about improved health and keys to the game.

Lake Brantley coach, Bob Peterson had focused on the role forward David Thomas would have to play in a Seminole victory against Tampa Robinson. Peterson's all-conference guard Doug Dershimer commented on what a premier player Tribe forward Bruce McCray had been all season long and how a few breaks, either way, could decide things at this stage of the season.

In the space of 24 hours, those comments would come straight back into play.

Late Thursday afternoon, just before their final practice walk-through for Tampa Robinson, Payne was about to start practice when Keith Whitney and David Thomas were horsing around in the gym. They engaged in a high-energy mock slap fight. Thomas made a sudden pivot to avoid a fake slap from Whitney when

222

Whitney accidentally stepped on Thomas' foot, pinning the forward's leg to an immobile position on the gym floor. Something popped in Thomas' knee, and he was forced to sit out of the practice. At the moment, Payne was not necessarily overly concerned.

By game day Friday morning, Thomas' knee had swollen to the size of a watermelon, and he had a pronounced limp. By Friday afternoon he was walking with the aid of a cane. By Friday night he would be in civilian clothes on the Tribe bench instead of crashing the boards against the tall and talented Knights.

Yet another dark cloud crept over the Seminoles' skyline. While the team had indeed been on the rebound from a bout with the flu, leading scorer Bruce McCray had contracted a case of bronchitis. He arrived in Lakeland having accidentally left his pocket inhaler behind in Sanford. He had intermittently used the inhaler during the season to battle an occasional bout of asthma. By game time, before the jump ball went up between the Sanford Seminoles and Tampa Robinson Knights, his breathing had become like trying to suck air through wet cement.

CHAPTER 27

No Backing Down

Sometimes, the Basketball Gods smile upon you. At other times they frown.

Sometimes in life, you catch a break, and sometimes the break catches you.

It would be an easy temptation to look back on that Friday night, March 14 in Lakeland, and dig deep for a pocket full of cliches. Rationales and second-guessing trademarks like, "what might have been, what could have been, what should have been, and what ifs" were readily at hand.

The Lakeland Civic Center's 8-thousand-plus seats were half-filled with the fannies of prep basketball fans from around the state and a rowdy and supportive crowd was in full voice for the Fighting Seminoles and Tampa Robinson Knights. They came for a game worthy of a Class 4-A state tournament semi-final. Tampa Robinson and Sanford Seminole ensured they got it. I would write one more Page 1 Above the Fold story that season. And the next day's *Sanford Herald* would carry the headline:

Proud Seminoles Gave It Their Best Shot

Seminole High's dream of a state basketball championship came to an end Friday night in Lakeland, but not without one of the most spirited comeback bids in state tournament history.

Playing without the services of starting forward David Thomas, and slowed by a sick Bruce McCray, Bill Payne's Fighting Seminoles rebounded off the floor from a 17-point deficit in the third quarter before bowing out to Tampa Robinson 76-73.

The loss ended a spectacular Tribe season, closing the record books on a 31-3 slate, a season that entered the Seminoles in the history books as the best-ever team from Seminole County.

"I'm proud of the kids and what they accomplished this year," said Payne of the Seminole's season.

"We could have folded easily tonight with David out and Bruce sick, but the kids reached down and battled all the way."

Among the many accomplishments the Tribe collected was the best-ever record for a Seminole County team and the District 9, Region 5, Section 3, Rotary Invitational, and Oviedo-Outlook Invitational titles to its list of credits.

School records and individual records fell by the wayside as the Tribe forged its finest season in history and represented the Five Star Conference for the first time in state tournament play. More on the Seminoles on Page 1B.

Sam Cook's inside lead sports page story reflected Tampa Robinson's efforts to bury the Fighting Seminoles with a big first half. It would also detail how the Tribe would not go quietly into the night. His game wrap carried the headline:

Tampa Robinson Tombstones Tribe 76-73

(Lakeland)—Tampa Robinson read the final will and testament to Sanford's Fighting Seminoles in the State 4-A Basketball tournament Friday night at the Lakeland Civic Center.

The tombstone was inscribed Robinson 76 Sanford 73. Put to rest with the Tribe was a final 31-3 season, the most victories in the history of Seminole County.

Included were FIVE championship trophies. The pride of coach Bill

225

Payne won the Rotary Bowl Tournament, the Lion Christmas Invitational, and the district, regional and sectional titles.

Friday night, however, the game Seminoles started with one foot in the grave. That foot, or rather a knee, belonged to the Tribe's splendid senior 6-4 David Thomas.

Thomas, the Seminole's jack-of-all-trades on the basketball court, injured some cartilage in his knee and was unable to dress out.

"I tried to pick 'em up from the bench," 6-4 Thomas said while tapping his cane lightly in a somber Seminole locker room. "But it just wasn't the same as being out there."

Thomas' absence became immediately apparent as Sanford turned the ball over six times in the first quarter as Robinson jumped to a 21-12 advantage.

After senior guard Glenn Stambaugh connected for two of his 23 points to bring Sanford within 11-9, the Tribe bench was hit with a technical.

Robinson point guard Tim Wheless connected on both free throws which prompted a run of eight straight points by the Knights.

Six-four junior Charlie Bradley, who coach Herman Valdes compares favorably to a former Robinson All-Star Herbie Allen, connected on three medium jump shots to spurt the Knights ahead in the last minute of the quarter.

Forward Bruce McCray finally notched two free throws with 31 seconds showing, but the trend had been set. Senior John Brumfield tipped in a shot at the buzzer for the nine-point edge.

"We try and tell our guys to bat the ball away with little time left," a disconsolate Bill Payne said about the two buzzer shots which

ended up being the margin of victory. Robinson meets Pensacola Washington tonight for the 4-A title.

The last-second tip-ins hurt Sanford again in the second quarter as Bradley and Sly James extended the lead to 14 points.

The quarter started well for the Tribe as McCray hit a jumper, and Willie White scored off a steal on the press to pull Sanford within 23-16.

The 6-3 Brumfield though, tipped in a missed free throw with two minutes to go for a 10-point lead. After James hit two free throws to offset a Stambaugh bucket, Brumfield banked in his rebound shot with one second showing for a 39-25 halftime bulge.

"Things weren't clicking," assessed Stambaugh about the lackluster first 16 minutes.

"I guess it could have been David (Thomas). We've started the same men for 33 games, you get used to each other. I guess it was just that missing link."

Missing link or whatever, the Tribe converted only 10 of 32 first-half shots for 33 percent. Add to that 5-of-9 free throws for 25 points.

Robinson meanwhile hit 15-of-29 floor shots for 52 percent and 7-of-16 free throws.

"They were 10-of-32 in the first half," Valdes reaffirmed.

"I knew they weren't going to shoot that poorly in the second half."

The Seminoles further compounded their troubles when 6-6 Reggie Butler picked up his third and fourth fouls early in the second half, and McCray was sidelined with another bronchitis attack.

With two starters sidelined Robinson appeared to be administering last rites when they jumped to a huge 50-33 lead on two free throws by James and two buckets by Brumfield, the last on a nifty steal and slam dunk.

The Seminoles, however, came fighting back from the premature burial behind the oxygen-revived McCray and the gutty performance by Stambaugh.

"For me, I just reached down. We were talking about pride at halftime," disclosed Stambaugh.

"If we're going to lose, we're not going to lose by 15. We just said we're not going to let our man score. It seems when we play better defense, our offense comes," directed Stambaugh.

That did it. Trailing by 17, guard Joe Baker hustled the Tribe a couple of steals while Stambaugh and McCray did the rest.

The 6-4 McCray, who revived for 27 points, hit a fadeaway jumper, which 6-5 substitute center Steve Grace followed up with a bucket as did Stambaugh to pull Sanford within 50-41 with 2:20 to play in the third period.

"I couldn't breathe out there," McCray said about the first half bronchitis problem. At halftime, they took me back and gave me some oxygen which helped."

While the oxygen assisted McCray, it also breathed life into the Tribe during a mad rush early in the fourth period.

Trailing 52-47 entering the quarter, Baker and McCray offset four Robinson free throws with baskets to make it 56-49 Knights.

McCray then grabbed a loose ball, broke for the basket, scored, and was fouled. He calmly converted the free toss to pull the Tribe

228

within 56-54 and still had 6:44 to play.

At this point, however, the vultures began to circle as the Knights regrouped from a spot they seemed to cherish all night—the free throw line.

"We shot 70 percent from the line for the year," senior James pointed out.

"We knew we'd be all right from there.

James personally took care of the death march himself. After connecting on a free throw, James helped out on a Stambaugh double team and broke free for a slam dunk and a 59-54 advantage.

Next, he worsened the Sanford condition with four straight free tosses to which the 5-11 Wheless added two more for a 64-56 margin with five minutes left to play.

During a two-minute surge by Tampa, Sanford could muster only one basket—by McCray—in its attempt to overtake the hearse.

Robinson connected on 26-of-34 free throws for the game including 16-of-21 in the crucial fourth quarter.

With three-quarters of the Tribe entombed, Sanford staged its last grasp at life when Butler hit with 1:27 left for a 70-67 ball game.

Brumfield, however, added a basket and Wheless two free throws to pump it to 74-67. The Tribe still wasn't dead.

Shun Thomas banked in a jumper, and Stambaugh added another six seconds later to make it 74-71 with 27 seconds remaining in the game.

Sixth-man Darrel Patterson finally pulled the plug on the fighting-for-life Tribe though, when he connected on both ends of a one-on-one for a 76-71 lead and only 17 ticks left. Butler added a final

Seminole bucket with 10 seconds to go.

"When you come this far, it's hard to make up the difference (17) points against a good team," said Stambaugh.

"They're a classy team, and we just couldn't get over the hump."

Hump or not, a pretty classy team went to its final resting place Friday night.

And so, it was over. When the final buzzer against Tampa Robinson went off in the Lakeland Civic Center, Seminole High's quest for a first-ever state championship ended. But the mood in the locker room following the game was not somber, or angry, or remorseful. Almost to a man, each player seemed comfortable in the sense that they had entered the battle, fought their best, even given the late circumstances leading up to the game, and left everything they had on the court.

The 80-mile drive over I-4-East from Lakeland back to Sanford was the shortest road trip of the Tribe's post-season run. And it gave me 90 minutes to contemplate the final column I would write about their chase for a state title.

I wanted it to accurately reflect the culmination of their season and their final battle that ended three points shy. The headline read:

State Tournament: The Stuff Dreams Are Made Of

State basketball championships. The stuff dreams are made of.

Bill Payne's Fighting Seminoles did a lot more than just dream about the state tournament this year.

They battled their way through regular season play, the district, regional and sectional competition to arrive at the doorstep of Lakeland.

But more than victories, rebounds, points, and assists, perhaps the Tribe's greatest accomplishment was growth. Not only as basketball players but also as young men.

Few teams make it to Lakeland for the Final Four. Fewer still go home state champions. But when the Tribe's vans rolled into Seminole High's parking lot at 1 a.m. Saturday morning, Seminole players came home as champions in their own right.

They didn't win the title, but they'll have some fantastic memories of this season to reminisce about with their grandchildren years from now when the reflexes and jump shots are dusty.

Memories: The perfect illustration of the drama and emotion of sports. Especially for high school-aged athletes.

"I don't think there's any one thing that will stick out in my mind about this season," reflected a drained Tribe coach Bill Payne.

"There were so many little things that happened this year to make it all happen for us. I will remember the work, the dedication, and the guts of the kids that played for me this year. That's something that will stay with me forever."

Payne's toughest assignment of the night might not have been handling the loss and consoling his players but explaining why it was all over to his teary-eyed four-year-old daughter Lisa in the parking lot.

The 6-4 coach gently cradled his bundle of joy and tried to explain losing to his young child.

231

"Somebody has to win, and somebody has to lose," he said softly. "Maybe next time will be our turn. We tried."

"I'll remember how proud I am of these guys tonight," said an injury-sidelined David Thomas.

"They never gave up. They kept coming back for more and more. I'm just proud of them. That's all I can say right now."

The salty-eyed senior, with disappointment etched on his face. added, "Nobody can take the 31 wins away from us. I think we have the best team in the state of Florida to be able to come back like that."

Senior Glenn Stambaugh echoed Thomas' remarks.

"We knew they weren't 17 points better than us. We had too much pride not to come back. I'm proud of this team, and nobody can take our 31 wins away. We couldn't get over the hump, but we never gave up."

"We had a chance to win it all," said a disappointed Reggie Butler.

"But I guess it just wasn't meant to be. I just want to thank God for the people, coach Payne and my teammates."

"I think this loss was hardest on David," commented "Big Bird" Steve Grace.

"He wanted to be in there with us so much. But we came farther this year than anybody thought we could."

Grace will be back next year.

Seldom used Joe Baker, forced off the bench due to foul trouble and injury, explained his role in the ball game.

"I just wanted to come in and do a good job, help these guys get

fired up. I wanted to win. In a game like this, you have only one chance. I thought we played a hell of a game. We had a hell of a season, and everybody gave more than 100 percent."

Bruce McCray, who battled bronchitis all night as well as leading the late charge talked about togetherness.

"I think playing without David affected us. We've put the same five guys out on the floor for 32 ball games coming in here. But I'm happy about the 31 wins. I just wish we could be coming back here Saturday night for one more game. I'm proud, and I'll remember how this team stuck together not just tonight but during the whole season."

"I feel great about coming this far," said Keith Whitney afterward.

"When we started together this season, we knew we wanted to make it to the state tournament.

"I'll remember all the good players on this team, the good guys we had on the bench, and the good times we all had together."

The southpaw guard added, "We played 33 games with David in the lineup. It made a difference tonight without him. But look at the job our bench did. They came in and did a great job."

Payne perhaps said it best though when he talked about all the little things adding up.

There were the two tough losses to Mainland and then the Tribe bounced back off the verge of another defeat to finally score their most important win of the year.

From this corner, the victory over the Buccaneers was the toughest mental accomplishment for the Seminoles of the season. It was in that game that Payne and his Tribe found out what they were truly made of.

Of course, speculation and the word "if" probably come into focus more in sports than in many places. What if David Thomas hadn't been injured? What if Bruce McCray hadn't been slowed by bronchitis?

But the Seminoles were too classy a team to make excuses for this season, and none are necessary.

Their records and accomplishments speak for themselves. From a media standpoint, there will be a few memories of this basketball season too. Refreshing in a business that sometimes becomes a little sardonic and downbeat, often negative too.

And when one stops to remember that these are 17 and 18-year-old kids, what they've accomplished and the pressure they've handled is impressive.

Undoubtedly it will be a long, long time before Seminole or any other prep team in Seminole County has a season like this.

That's the stuff dreams are made of.

CHAPTER 28
Epilogue

Forty-two years is a long time to carry around memories. But I always knew that at some point, when time permitted, I would return to that remarkable 1979-80 season of Sanford Seminole High basketball and commit those memories to paper. And in September 2022, the ingredients for transforming those recollections into a narrative began to take shape.

But before I could begin working on the transcript for the book that would become "Three Points Shy," I had to kick off the cobwebs of events that took place more than four decades ago and do some journalistic homework.

For years I had carted around tear sheet copies of all the stories I compiled about the Tribe's incredible run. But in 1999, I moved back to Alaska, and there was just no room to pack them in a vehicle for a 5,287-mile ride from Winter Park, Florida, to Anchorage and eventually Kodiak Island. Into the dumpster they went.

So, in the Spring of 2022, I returned to Sanford and walked back into the offices of *The Sanford Herald,* hoping to peruse what had at one time been hard-bound copies of each edition of the newspaper dating back even further than the 70s and 80s.

The first person to greet me was ace photographer Tommy Vincent, still with the Santa Claus beard and Paul Newman's baby blue eyes. Tommy still shoots for the newspaper, and with the consolidation of the newspaper industry over the past few decades, he also wears half-a-dozen other hats as well.

Unfortunately, Vincent informed me that with ownership changes of the publication over the years, the hard-bound copies went by the wayside and were nowhere to be found. But Vincent was a walking encyclopedia of information and pointed me in the direction of the Museum of Seminole County History in Sanford, which stored decades of past issues on microfilm.

The museum's coordinator, Bennett Lloyd, was extremely helpful in assisting my search for the information vital to the book. It was during that walk back through the pages of the 1979-80 *Sanford Herald* that I really rediscovered just how intertwined the experiences and careers of some of the people and places of that year would become.

Reflecting and projecting forward, it was like the three rivers in my home state of Pennsylvania that meet in Pittsburgh: the Allegheny, the Monongahela, and Ohio.

Just a few examples of how paths and storylines crossed and intermingled:

Young Benton Wood, a junior at Lyman High that year and the youngest on our sports staff, would continue to write for the newspaper until he graduated, then attended the University of Florida as a journalism major and returned to Central Florida to be hired by the *Orlando Sentinel* as a sportswriter.

He would eventually discover the error of his ways, depart the journalism landscape, and follow in his father's footsteps into the legal profession. Now a graduate of Miami Law School, he resides in Orlando and works as a partner in the law firm of Fisher Phillips, specializing in Labor and Employment law.

He still reads the sports section first every morning and over the years has provided legal representation for virtually every municipality in Seminole County including the City of Sanford and Seminole County itself.

"I remember two things most about that basketball season of '79-80," reflects Wood.

"First, Stambaugh was the perfect fit for Seminole High that year. Seminole had great leapers and could run. Stambaugh, with his shooting and ballhandling, was the finishing piece to a great team."

"Second," recalls the sportswriter-turned-attorney, "is coach Bill Payne.

"Here I was, a cub reporter still in high school, and Bill Payne could not have been kinder. He treated me like a professional. And not just for interviews and game stories. He was an incredible basketball scholar and would take the time to talk to me about things that never would show up within game stories. He was willing to talk at length about the strategy of breaking down a full-court press, or a zone defense. Back in the late 70s, a lot of high school coaches took those positions for the salary supplement. Payne took it because he not only loved coaching but worked at making the coaching profession more professional."

It was Sam Cook who recruited Wood as a member of our staff. Sam would succeed me as sports editor when I departed in the Spring of 1982 for a broadcasting and public relations position with the Erie Cardinals, in my hometown of Erie., Pa. I would trade late-night bus rides around Central Florida chasing sports stories for late-night bus rides, cheap hotels, and midnight concession stand hot dogs that passed for dinner in the glamorous life of Class-A Minor League Baseball in the New York-Penn League. Even in the Finger Lakes region of New York, I stumbled across another Seminole County connection. Young Dave Martinez, a star outfielder for the Lake Howell Silver Hawks, was quickly rising through the ranks of the Chicago Cubs farm system. We bumped into each other during a game when Erie's Cardinals were playing Martinez's Batavia Cubs. Dave killed my team that night, going four-for-five at the plate and collecting seven RBIs. He would go on to have a solid Major League career and manage the Washington Nationals.

Sam not only found great sports stories at Seminole High. He also found a bride. His wife Gayle taught alongside Bill Payne and coached the Tribe's cheerleading team for several seasons.

Sam would remain sports editor for *The Sanford Herald* until 1988. He took part in a unique three-month sports internship with *USA Today* and then was hired on as a sportswriter with the *Ft. Myers News Press*. He transitioned into news and would go on to become an award-winning columnist for the publication.

We have remained friends over the years, and Sam has been kind enough to write the foreword for "Three Points Shy."

One of the last stories I would file before my departure would be on the retirement of Joe Sterling as head basketball coach at Seminole Community College. Sterling would stay on for some time as Athletic Director and be instrumental in hiring his coaching successor.

One of the first stories Sam would write with his new title would be the hiring of Bill Payne to succeed Sterling.

When I visited the newspaper in search of hard-bound back issues from '79-80, sitting in the office right next to Tommy Vincent was statistician extraordinaire Dean Smith. Smith followed Payne to Seminole Community College for several seasons and began stringing part-time for the sports department of *The Sanford Herald*. He went full-time with the newspaper in 1990 and was named sports editor in 1992. He continues to wear two hats as a scoreboard operator and statistician for many of the men's and women's sports programs at the University of Central Florida.

Smith had a front-row seat for that 1979-80 season, perched at Payne's right elbow for every minute of their record-breaking run. Two things stand out in his memory of that 31-3 season.

"The first thing that comes to mind about that team was that they never panicked. It didn't matter what the score was, what the situation was, or how much or little time was on the clock.

They just had an incredible amount of confidence in themselves that they were going to win."

While still coaching at Seminole Community College, Joe Sterling did, in fact, put a bug in Payne's ear numerous times over the course of Seminole High's 79-80 season. He wanted to recruit all five of the Tribe's starters to continue their basketball days at the two-year junior college. And he came close. Bruce McCray, Reggie Butler, Keith Whitney, and David Thomas signed on with SCC and went on to have varying degrees of post-high school success. The fifth starter, slick-shooting Glenn Stambaugh, stayed close to home as well. He signed on with Division II Rollins College in nearby Winter Park. Sterling also managed to recruit Lake Howell's high-scoring forward Reggie Barnes and Lake Brantley's All-Conference guard Doug Dershimer to his 1980-81 roster at SCC, giving the junior college a robust representation of Seminole County prep talent.

Thomas ran into off-court issues and would not make it to SCC. Butler played for two seasons. McCray and Whitney took interesting paths following their two years of playing for Joe Sterling.

Bill Payne told me jokingly numerous times during '79-80 about

Bruce McCray's ability to score.

"With his collection of unorthodox shots, Bruce is going to score 20 in high school, he'll score 20 in college, and probably 20 if he makes it to the NBA. Bruce is going to get Bruce's points."

McCray continued his scoring prowess during his two years at SCC. But unfortunately, I was unable to precisely check on Payne's prediction of Bruce getting 20 points a game there. When I returned to Central Florida in 2010, I was hired on as an adjunct communications instructor at SCC. One of my first stops on campus during my first semester there was to see if the gym, the House Joe Sterling built, still carried the magical vibes of the prep basketball tournaments held there. I was genuinely disappointed to walk into the facility and find the gym hollow of any athletic activity. The once burgeoning trophy case filled with gleaming hardware of championships and awards was neglected and covered in dust. I was even more disappointed to discover that SCC had dropped its basketball program. And like the missing hardbound copies of *The Sanford Herald*, nearly all the records and documentation once stored in the school's Sports Information Department had gone missing as well, save for a sprinkling of a handful of prior seasons media guides.

 McCray completed his college career at Bluefield State College in Bluefield. West Va., just a stone's throw from the Virginia State line.

And somehow, those closed-door "come-to-Jesus" meetings Seminole High assistant principal Lamar Richardson had with McCray during his sophomore year of high school took root and ran deep.

Upon graduation from Bluefield State, McCray returned home to

Seminole County and spent time as a teacher and coach for Seminole County Public Schools.

Somehow, someway, speedy point guard and left-handed whiz Keith Whitney parlayed his time at SCC into a roster spot literally 4,739 miles away. Whitney made his way to tiny Chaminade University in Honolulu. It was in 1982 that the Silverswords gained national notoriety and shocked the college basketball universe when the NAIA school knocked off top-ranked Virginia with Ralph Sampson at the center by a score of 77-72 in a December 1982 Christmas tournament.

Whitney canned a game-winning 20-foot jump shot with no time on the clock in December of 1984 as Chaminade played giant killers once again, this time beating fourth-ranked and undefeated Southern Methodist University 71-70 in the same Christmas tournament.

As for the sweet-shooting Stambaugh, who was always pure money from 25 feet out and even more so from the foul line? He played four seasons for the Rollins College Division II Tars and, at one point, held the school record for most career games played. Stambaugh averaged just over seven points a game during his four-year career with Rollins. He earned a B.S. in Business and Economics. He's still money. Literally, as Senior Vice President/ Commercial Dealer Services for Truist Bank in Jacksonville, Fl.

Stephen "Big Bird" Grace, who provided quality minutes at center and off the bench that season as a junior, earned an appointment to the U.S. Naval Academy following his senior year at Seminole High. He suited up for the Midshipmen his freshman year appearing in four games. He went on to earn a B.S. in Physical Science from the military service academy.

241

Shun Thomas, the team's invaluable sixth man off the bench, would enlist in the U.S. Army following graduation and spend time stationed in Germany.

And #20 Mike Gaudreau, the backup guard who selflessly volunteered his jersey so that Glenn Stambaugh could be in the lineup to hit the winning foul shots against Apopka in the semi-final of the District 9 tournament? Foul shots that literally saved the Tribe's season and set up the crucial third game against Mainland. Gaudreau graduated a year later in 1981 but continued to bleed the school colors of orange and black for years to come. He would return to Seminole High first as an assistant principal, then was named the school's principal in February 2007.

Gaudreau's seasons as a basketball player when the Tribe rescued victory from the jaws of defeat prepared the principal well. Gaudreau helped transform Seminole High into earning an "A" School ranking and was on hand throughout the 2008 football season when Sanford's Seminoles did in fact win a state championship in football. By 2008, Sanford Seminole had moved up to Class 6-A status and trailed Miami Northeast 21-0 after the first quarter. As his basketball team had done so often in 1979-80, the Fighting Seminoles fought back in football too, scoring 28 unanswered points and winning the game when Tribe quarterback Ray Ray Armstrong connected with Andre Debose on a 40-yard bomb with just 33 seconds left to win the game for Seminole 28-21.

Bill Payne's coaching success that year at Seminole High was a harbinger of things to come. He would spend two more years with the high school before accepting the head coaching job at Seminole Community College following the retirement of program-founding coach Joe Sterling.

Payne would spend 22 years at the junior college level with coaching stops following SCC at St. Petersburg Junior College and Caldwell Community College & Technical Institute in North Carolina. He would compile an impressive junior college coaching resume of 443 wins against 221 losses.

After that memorable 1980 season, Payne told me there was no single thing that stood out from the 31-3 run. When we reconnected in the Winter of 2022, as "Three Points Shy" was being written, his thoughts had shifted slightly. And I thank his wife, Barbara, for letting me steal him for frequent Sunday phone conversations to compare notes and memories on a story 42 years in the making.

"I recall three things that do stand out about that season," confirms Payne.

"The first is the kids. They were just such a great bunch. They worked so hard over those three years, every one of them—the starters and the reserves. They played together, they were friends together, they pushed each other in practice, and they had pride. You never want your season to end, and you always hope to have one more game to play. But there are absolutely no regrets."

Payne says the second thing he recalls is the magical ride the team took the community on during the season.

"I think the team really brought out the best in the Sanford Community. As the season went on, things just kept building and building and all of Sanford was caught up in the streak, the games against Mainland, and the playoff run. It really was something to see. You could go anywhere in town that season, and the whole town was talking about the basketball team."

And finally, the third thing that stands out in his now 42-year-old

243

recollection of that run: backup guard Mike Gaudreau, his junior reserve who sacrificed his jersey #20 so that Glenn Stambaugh could suit up in the District-9 tournament opening round game against Apopka.

"That was an incredible act by Mike. That was huge for a young kid to give up his uniform on that night. Mike Gaudreau literally saved our season," reflected Payne in one of our concluding phone calls.

In the late 1970s and early 1980s, playing for your high school team was still a big thing for many kids. They considered it an honor to try out, earn a jersey, earn a spot, and be on a team. And covering Seminole County sports during that period was a joy as well.

We were a small newspaper and a young sports staff. But every step of the way, the coaches, athletic directors, and many of the principals, as well as the athletes we covered, were supportive. Our phone calls were always returned, they always made time for pre-and-post-game interviews, and collectively they made game nights and pizza at midnight in the newsroom, treasured slices of time.

The ups and downs, the wins and losses, the highs and lows, and the myriad of people part of that season all converged to create a memorable basketball journey. Even if it did conclude three points shy.

About the Author

A Navy "brat" who bounced around the globe, Joe DeSantis has been writing sports and news since his junior year at Kellam High School in Virginia Beach.

DeSantis holds a B.A. in Speech Communications and an M.A. in Communication Studies from Edinboro University of Pennsylvania.

An Army veteran and graduate of the Department of Defense Information Schools, he earned dual Military Occupation Specialties as a Public Information Specialist and Military Broadcast Specialist. DeSantis was initially stationed with the 1st Armored Division in Ansbach, Germany, then later as Senior Sports Announcer

245

and Writer with American Forces Network-Europe, Frankfurt, Germany.

The author has held various media positions including sports editor, staff writer, radio station news/program director and morning anchor, newspaper managing editor as well as high school and college level communications instructor.

DeSantis has done network-level broadcast news for both NBC and ABC and has broken national news stories of former New Hampshire Governor John Sununu's appointment as White House Chief of Staff for President George H. W. Bush, and of David Souter's nomination to the United States Supreme Court.

An avid baseball fan, DeSantis is a long-suffering Boston Red Sox fanatic.

This is his first novel.